STATE OF MIND 2.0

11 Lessons of the Most Productive People on the Planet

CHRISTOPHER A. PINCKLEY

ABOUT THE AUTHOR

CHRIS is a coach & consultant who's area of expertise continually defies brackets, labels, or usual definitions. If you were to combine leadership development, expansion of mental capacity, enhanced self awareness of social behaviors, and the ending self sabotage cycles, then you would be getting close. Chris has been referred to as an executive coach, an integral coach, a leadership coach, and even a mindfulness coach. Whatever the case, he has yet to work with an individual or a team who didn't come away from their time together without radical expansion of consciousness in worldview, business, and self awareness. Chris will help you to:

- Streamline your thinking to create a mental laser focus that has a 10x effect upon your action-steps

- Create solid boundaries so that you protect your valuable time and energy and never waste another second

- Operate from stillness so that your ability to utilize creativity in problem solving is optimized

- Develop a plan of action to effectively achieve your larger than life vision

- Build the state of mind necessary to occupy a page in the history books and create a positive global impact

Chris has written and rewritten over 20 books, produced 3 podcasts, and written over 400 articles. He has worked with dozens of amazing individuals in a one on one or team setting. He does the majority of his work from his home in Northern California via video. When he is not writing, coaching, or speaking, then he is meditating, hiking in the mountains, or spending time with his beautiful life partner and her two angels.

www.christopherpinckley.com

TABLE OF CONTENTS

About the Author iii

Introduction 1

Lesson 1: Imagination is More Important than Reality............. 4

Rules of the Imagination 6

   1. Never Study the Data 7

   2. Never Follow the Trends.. 11

   3. Visualize, Believe, and Feel... 15

Lesson 1: Integration.. 18

Lesson 2: Focus on the One Thing.. 19

Rules of Focus 21

   1. Decide What One Thing is Most Important
      to You and Never Deviate... 22

   2. Dedicate Yourself to Obsessively Learning
      About the One Thing 26

   3. Be the Best at the One Thing That You
      Possibly Can 29

Lesson 2: Integration.. 32

Lesson 3: Self-Discipline...33

Rules of Discipline...35

    1.   Show Up and Do the work 36

    2.   Never Celebrate Before it's Accomplished..................40

    3.   Adhere to a Daily Routine...44

Lesson 3: Integration..48

Lesson 4: Control Your Environment.............................49

Rules of Environment 51

    1.   Never Have Anyone in Your Circle Who Doesn't
       Hold You to the Highest 52

    2.   Create the External Circumstances Under Which
       You Work Best..54

    3.   Keep Both Your Home and Your Work
       Environment Organized 57

Lesson 4: Integration..60

Lesson 5: Boundaries 61

Rules of Boundaries 64

    1.   Never Allow Anyone to Keep You from
       Your Work..65

    2.   Never Allow Someone to Project Their Limitation
       onto You...70

    3.   Never Let Yourself Get Drawn into Drama.................75

Lesson 5: Integration..79

Lesson 6: Focus on the Solution, Not the Problem 80

Rules of the Solution 82

1. Never Complain About the Woes of the world 83

2. Focus Your Attention Upon Creating Solutions 86

3. Understanding What You Don't Want Helps
    You to Understand
    What You Do Want 90

Lesson 6: Integration 95

RATE YOUR CURRENT LIKELIHOOD
OF MAKING HISTORY 96

Lesson 7: Operate From Stillness 102

Rules of Stillness 106

1. Do Not Overthink the Situation 107

2. Get Quiet and Withdraw From the Workplace 111

3. Wait for the Next Right Move 114

Lesson 7: Integration 117

Lesson 8: Be Yourself.. 119

Rules of You.. 122

1. Do Not Compare Yourself to Other People 123

2. Do Not Judge Yourself by Your Competition............ 127

3. Stay True to Your Own Creative Flow 131

Lesson 8: Integration 134

Lesson 9: It Will Happen When it's Ready to Happen........... 136

Rules of When.. 138

   1.   It Doesn't Happen When You Want it to happen 139

   2.   Don't get caught up in the numbers........................... 143

   3.   Stay Nonattached to the Outcome............................. 147

Lesson 9: Integration.. 152

Lesson 10: Never Give Up 154

Rules of Never Give Up.. 158

   1.   A Failure is an Opportunity to Learn....................... 159

   2.   Changing Your Approach is Okay.............................. 161

   3.   The Last Leg of the Journey....................................... 164

Lesson 10: Integration.. 168

Lesson 11: You Are Never Done Creating.................... 169

Rules of Never Getting it Done.................................... 172

   1.   Retirement is Never the Goal..................................... 173

   2.   You Continue to Develop New Ideas 175

   3.   If You Do Master One Craft, Move on to
      the Next.. 177

Lesson 11: Integration.. 181

INTRODUCTION

Productivity. Merriam-Webster defines it as "yielding results, benefits, or profits," which will comprise a small part of what we're going to talk about in this book. What we're really going to focus on is the *state of productivity*. In other words, we're going to examine what it takes to be able to continually yield results, benefits, or profits. Since every single person reading these words has achieved at least one result in their life, then the question upon which we will focus isn't how to produce something. Rather, the question that we need to answer is *how do you develop the ability to stay productive long enough to achieve something of great significance?*

As it turns out, there is a formula that virtually all of the most productive people on the planet use to maintain their state of productivity. The result of utilizing this powerful formula is that productivity is able to be maintained as a state of being or *state of mind.* This means that it's a gear you have the ability to shift into and even maintain if that is your desire.

It's great news for those of us who are not yet billionaires or world famous. It means that, if you really want to be, you can be. It's as simple as following this formula until you arrive at your destination. Interestingly, part of the equation is that you never really quit being productive. You never quit solving problems or entertaining the people of the world. It's part of the secret to the formula and the ability to shift into this state of mind. It's that you actually love being productive so much that you can't help but to continually stay productive.

Now the question becomes: is the *love of productivity* really a gear that you can shift into? You bet it is. Every characteristic, habit, or trait can be learned or trained if you have the desire to learn it, practice it, or be it. Follow the formula, lesson by lesson, and you will arrive at the same state of mind as that of the most productive people on the planet.

When I think of the most productive people on the planet I think of names like Jean Paul DeJoria, Debbi Fields, Curtis Jackson, Warren Buffett, Stephen King, Barbara Streisand, Richard Branson, Danica Patrick, Will Smith, Tiger Woods, J.K. Rowling, Ray Dalio, Michael Phelps, Floyd Mayweather, Sylvester Stallone, Robert Johnson, Michael Gerber, Elon Musk, Kobe Bryant, Martha Stewart, Tim Ferris, Shawn Carter, Christian Von Koenigsegg, and Oprah Winfrey.

How did they do it? They followed this very formula to achieve world caliber success like nobody has ever seen.

Do you want to make history? If so, you are reading the right book. Follow this formula as if your life depended on it and you will rise to the top 0.1% of the highest level achievers in the world. But, you must engage with the lessons in this book in order to achieve that kind of uncommon result.

This formula functions in an exponential model.

- If you put in 10% effort you will get a 0% return.
- If you put in 25% effort you will get a 2.5% return.
- If you put in 50% effort you will get a 5% return.

- If you put in 75% effort you will get a 7.5% return.

- If you put in 99% effort you will get a 10% return.

- If you put in 100% effort and fully commit to this formula you will get a 10,000% return.

You may be tempted to think that I'm crazy or making it all up. And yet, in this instance, I am only reporting the news. I am simply disseminating something to the world that has been long overdue. Strictly speaking: I'm just the messenger. There is a reason why so few people achieve world caliber status and are considered by general consensus to be the most productive people on planet. It's because it requires you to go "all in" and this is the most difficult thing for the average person to do.

It's easy to read a book and apply a lesson or two. But it's incredibly difficult to fully commit yourself to following and adhering to a set of principles for days, weeks, months, and years to come.

So I ask you: do you have what it takes?

Let's find out.

Lesson 1

IMAGINATION IS MORE IMPORTANT THAN REALITY

"Imagination is more important than knowledge. For knowledge is limited to all we know and understand, while imagination embraces the entire world, and all there will ever be to know and understand."

—Albert Einstein

The first and most important lesson to learn is the immense value of your own imagination. Most people vastly underestimate the power of their imagination or auto-associate it with the act of daydreaming. Imagination is generally relegated to the couch dreamer who spends the majority of their free time sitting on a couch dreaming about the "what ifs" of a life unlived. It's true that the average person uses or, I should say, *misuses* their imagination in this manner.

It reminds me of the scene from the movie *Dumb and Dumber* when they begin using $100 bills to wipe their noses. Most people wipe their noses with their imagination and completely miss the treasure trove of ideas and innovations waiting to be mined from within.

Rather, your imagination is the key to your ability to tap into limitless creativity and innovation, as well as your reason for being. Within your imagination lie all of the ideas that are waiting for you to breathe life force into them and manifest them into the world. You have the ability to make this world a better place, whether it is to make people's lives easier through a product, to transport them into another dimension through your art, or to help them get the food they need to survive. Your imagination has all of that and a lot more within awaiting your acknowledgment of its existence.

RULES OF THE IMAGINATION

#1 Never Study the Data

Before attempting to access the wealth of limitless potential stored within your powerful imagination, you need to safeguard it against its enemies. Enemy number one of your imagination is data. Data. Data is the ultimate destructor of imagination and innovation.

Have you ever noticed that people who study data are about the least innovative, most pessimistic and boring people around? It's a sad but true statement that I would personally rather slap myself in the face with a brick than spend an hour with an analyst.

Here is what happens to people who study data for prolonged periods of time: imagination death. Yes, their imagination is destroyed, literally. If you believe that reality is created by analyzing data then you will never create anything new or contribute anything new to the world. If everyone lived this way then the world would come to a screeching halt. All technology and innovation and art would come to an abrupt end.

Here is why: studying what has happened before cannot create what is yet to come. Any time you analyze data you are always and only ever studying what "has been." Data cannot predict the future. Data is not the determinant of creativity, and thank god this is so. If it were, then we would all be in trouble. We would be in serious trouble because we would be studying and basing our future on the past. Can you imagine the insanity of it? If the Wright Brothers had studied the data then it would have told them that what they were trying to do was impossible. If it hasn't been done then the data can only tell the story of what is not yet possible. If you believe the story the data tells then you will never be known as an innovator.

Data only tells the story of what the world believed was possible yesterday. It does not, nor will it ever be able to predict what is possible in the future. Another way of saying this is that data cannot accurately predict the creative potential of the future innovators of the world. It's not to say that intelligent people can't make predictions about things that will come to pass on this planet. For instance, anyone can look at the way technology is moving and make an accurate prediction that we will all eventually have electric cars that can fly.

However, none of the greatest inventions or innovations in the world was determined by data. Personal computers and laptops were not determined by data. The song "Thriller" was not determined by data. Rousey's amazing win streak in the UFC was not determined by data. Netflix was not determined by data. Tesla Motors was not built on data.

The reason for this is that all of the greatest and most innovative ideas are completely new and foreign to the marketplace. Who would have ever thought that a pop-horror song would become the single most popular song of all time? Not me. Not you either. Nobody would have thought that. *Why?* The reason is that it can't be determined by data. This is because it comes from the imagination, which is beyond the realm of data.

Personal computers and laptops came from where? If you guessed the imagination then you guessed correctly. Something cannot be analyzed if it doesn't physically exist yet. It's like trying to analyze and study the effects of creating the wheel before you introduce it into the marketplace.

Ridiculous, right? And yet this is what people have become entrained into doing: seeking validation before they execute on their business, invention, or art by first analyzing the data.

I can only really think of one valid scenario for studying the marketplace data. This is if your passion is in startups, creating them, funding them, building them, etc. In other words, the act of building the startup is the passion itself for you, then analyzing the market to see if the product or service your startup is offering could be considered valid. The reason is that the act of analyzing the data is part of the game and the passion of the startup.

However, even then, if you want to rise to the top 0.1%, you may be asking for trouble. Remember, the most productive people on the planet do not study data; they build from their imagination.

Oprah Winfrey says there were one hundred other talk shows launched during her reign as talk show queen. Her team would often become concerned about the next new talk show being launched. She would say to them, "Don't worry about what they're doing, they're not us." She never paid any attention to what the competition was doing, ever. Her only response was to step up her own game and become a better version of herself.

And how did that work out for her? Right, exactly.

At the very instant you decide to study the data and analyze *what has been* you have just created a gap between yourself and the most productive people on the planet. This gap is represented by the amount of faith and belief you have in yourself. When you analyze data you are telling your own inner genius "I don't trust you, so I need to make sure that we're heading in the right direction." The world's most productive people inherently trust and believe in themselves and their creative flow. They never doubt their own inner genius, which means that they don't study the statistics or analyze the data.

Now, neither do you.

#2 Never Follow the Trends

What is a trend anyway? A trend is simply a well-worn path that was originally created by one person who thought differently than everybody else on the entire planet. In fact, this is the definition of every single trend in existence. Another way of saying this is that once it's a trend then everyone knows about it. In the beginning nobody knew about it because it was only an idea. One person brought this idea into existence by pushing hard for years and years until the universe relented and accepted it as a path. Once it became a path then people began to walk on it. Then they told their friends, and their friends told their friends. Then, overnight, it became known as a trend.

It's human nature to want to follow what's popular, what's working, and to always search for the well-worn path. However, this is not where the creativity, inspiration, and money lie. The money is where everyone else is not. If you walk down the well-worn path then you are going to be walking shoulder to shoulder with hundreds, thousands, and even millions of other people. If you desire to stand out then you need to strike out on your own. This may very well mean that you need to get out your machete, roll up your sleeves, and get ready for some work. All of the most productive people on the planet are well aware of this, having cut their own paths since the beginning of time.

Peter Thiel says that "trends are overrated" and I couldn't agree more. What happens is that you see someone doing something that you like and think "I could do that!" The problem is that someone else is already doing that and, if you are seeing it publically, then it probably means they are doing it quite well. It's one thing to get inspired by something that you see and have the desire to create your own version of it. It's quite another to attempt to closely model your idea or project after somebody else who is already doing it really well. You have fallen for the temptation to begin to adhere to what's popular or what's currently selling the most.

The world's most productive never, ever follow trends. They never try to do what has already been done and never try to emulate another person's idea.

If you want to be an innovator then you need to think far beyond trends. In fact, you need to think so far beyond trends that people think you are crazy for thinking what you think. This is where your pot of gold is. It's in "crazy." If people think that you are crazy, or that it can't be done, or that it is not a very good idea, then you may very well be close to the perfect idea.

Now if your idea was to build an electric car that competes with Tesla, well it might not be a great idea. This is because of the afore-mentioned concept that if somebody else is already doing it really well then it's not an original idea. What could be different is if you are thinking about innovating the electric car or giving it a new look. For instance, if your idea is to be the first ever automobile manufacturer to build cars that run solely on solar power, then it could potentially be a valid idea. Or, perhaps your idea is to create a unique style of electric car that integrates luxury as the primary selling point, thus enabling you to tap into an entirely new market of prospective buyers.

In the end it's only a good idea if you are passionate about it and not following a trend. In this specific example, you may actually be safe since there are not many electric car manufacturers in existence yet. Another way of saying this is that it's not yet a trend. It is not a well-worn path, but its time will come soon.

A positive aspect of observing other people who are successful is to allow them to inspire you. Thus, what *is* a positive byproduct of studying trend setters, disruptors, and innovators is to be inspired by the individuals who set them. This is perfectly healthy and even recommended. Sylvester Stallone was inspired by Chuck Wepner, who went 15 rounds with Muhammad Ali in 1975. What Stallone *did* do was to get really inspired and write a script about it called *Rocky*. What he *didn't* do was try to become a professional boxer.

See the difference?

This is how some of the most productive people on the planet use the achievements of others to inspire them to do or create something amazing. They will often purposefully seek out and study individuals who are inspiring to them to stimulate their own state of productivity. They may even get ideas from observing other high level achievers who are making big waves. However, they are never trying to copy or emulate. Rather, what they are seeking is inspiration to bolster their own creative flow. This is a completely different scenario from reading Larry Ellison's rag to riches story and deciding that you want to be the next software billionaire.

You may have been inspired by his story, but you are walking down the wrong path if you want to have his lifestyle and be the next software billionaire.

What would be different is if, prior to learning about his

story, you already had a vision of a new type of software in your mind that would revolutionize Silicon Valley. You happened to hear about his story and it lit the creative spark inside you that you needed in order to help you realize anything was possible. So you got to work immediately building your own, unique vision that was formed within your own, unique imagination. Ellison's story was just the juice to fire the engine, but it was not the engine itself.

Innovators are never followers. They are creators in the fullest sense, whether it is through art, business, education, or healthcare. Followers follow trends, trendsetters set them.

#3 Visualize, Believe, and Feel

Something that most people do not know about the most productive people on the planet is how they approach their vision. Their approach is not as cerebral as you might believe. There is a certain childlike innocence that goes into the mindset of the most productive people on the planet. It has to do with having a vision in their mind that excites them, believing that they can achieve this vision, and the ability to create the feeling ahead of time that accomplishing this vision would provide them.

Upon initial observation it may come across as a little woo-woo or impractical. Yet, at the heart of all of the most productive people on the planet, you will find this approach to creation. It's the belief that "I have already created it - you just don't see it yet." In the same way that Michelangelo would say that he could see the sculpture within, these amazing super achievers will tell you they can already see their dreams created within their minds. It's almost as if they exist in a fantasy world that only they can see. The fact that you can't see it or believe in it has zero bearing on their belief and faith that it will come to pass. In fact, they can see the visual image so clearly in their mind that it appears more real than reality.

What is real anyway? Have you ever challenged the notion of reality? Have you ever stopped to ask yourself if the life you are living is real? The value here is not to confuse or convolute your approach to life to the point where you sit and ponder the meaning of your existence. Instead, these questions are aimed at getting you to question the nature of your beliefs. *Do they really serve you?* If you think about it and, I mean take a very honest look at your life, then you may unearth something rather startling. This little nugget is that upon very close examination, most of the beliefs you have about reality are extremely limiting.

The most productive people on the planet have a tendency to either dismiss beliefs or continuously upgrade them. They do not accept what is or is not possible by societal standards. Instead, these ultra-productive maniacs have created their own set of beliefs. It goes something like this: *if I can imagine it, then I can build it, be it, or experience it.* Period. In other words, they rarely, if ever, accept what other people tell them about what can or can't be done. Trying to convince one of these folks about what can't be done and why not will probably only get the door shut in your face. Eventually, if you carry on, they will most likely disown you in any sort of association.

Why?

The world's most productive people do not accept the belief in limitation and neither should you. Never, ever accept somebody else's idea of limitation. To do so is to begin to limit your inner creative genius and put a chokehold on your own ability to innovate. The only reason you would do this is to either self-validate your own lack of desire to see it through to the end or to validate someone else's lack of desire to see you see it through to the end (so that you can validate your own lack of desire to see it through to the end). That's it, the only reason. So, is it a good enough reason to not achieve your dreams? Is there any reason good enough to not achieve your dreams?

Right, you see my point.

So unless your idea is to blow up the planet, there is no reason good enough not to follow through with going for what you want in this lifetime.

Lesson 1: Integration

1. Do not analyze the data. Nothing innovative ever came from it. It can't be an innovation if it isn't new. Analyzing the data is for people who want to play it safe. Playing it safe never made anyone into a billionaire or world famous, ever.

2. Never follow the trends. Unless you are a brainless lemming, you will want to steer clear of all trends. You cannot create a new path by following someone else's. Get out your machete and turn off the path right now, this instant. Begin cutting and eventually someone will follow you. If you keep cutting long enough then millions will follow you.

3. Begin to question the nature of reality. What is real? How do you know it is? What if you knew that you could create anything that you could imagine within your mind? Begin to do what all of the greatest innovators have done since the beginning of time: treat the vision in your mind as your only reality. Do this until everyone else can see it too.

Lesson 2

FOCUS ON THE ONE THING

"Most people have no idea of the giant capacity we can immediately command when we focus all of our resources on mastering a single area of our lives."

—Tony Robbins

This concept is probably the one that is the most underrated, overlooked, and difficult for people to follow. It's the idea of picking one thing, one idea and sticking with it to the bitter end. Most people just can't do it. I've thought long and hard about this problem that seems to perplex people.

Why is it so hard to pick one thing and stick with it?

Is it because of the growing tendency of mass media to create the need for instant gratification? Is it because it's difficult to find one thing that you are really passionate about? Is it because it's difficult to believe that you will ever be that good at it? Sure, all of these items could make choosing and deciding upon one direction a difficult task. But what is it really?

Here is my conclusion: fear. It's the fear that you are going to put all your eggs in one basket, it's not going to work out, you are going to waste years of your life in the process and wind up right back at zero.

Fear.

You may be tempted to think that's a pretty damn good reason to be afraid! It is and it isn't. It's always good to have a certain amount of fear in your life because it keeps you frosty. Fear can keep you from trying anything at all just for the sake of trying it. In other words, knowing that you do only have a certain amount of time on the planet can give you a healthy fear of not following the right direction. This means switching that fear around to work for you instead of against you. This means that, *yes,* you should fear wasting the minutes, hours, and days of your life on something that is a dead end.

Then the question is: *how do I know if it's a dead end?*

The answer is that you don't. You only actually know one thing about your idea: *whether you love it or not.* This is the only valid compass when it comes to decision time about the one thing that you should focus upon. It's the only way to know if your idea is valid or not, whether you love it or not. If you don't then, yes, maybe you should hold out for awhile and keep looking.

Whatever you do though, don't tolerate a yellow light in your life. It should either be *green* to go, or *red* to stop. Another way of saying this is to never allow your life to oscillate because you can't decide. The most productive people on the planet are powerful executioners who only see red or green. They either go or don't go. They don't spend years and years thinking about it. If they love it, chances are they have already pulled the trigger while everyone else is still pondering the meaning of life.

You may never figure out the meaning of life, but you can figure out a way to make everyone else's better. You do this by executing on one thing and being the absolute best you can be at it.

RULES OF FOCUS

#1 Decide What One Thing is Most Important to You and Never Deviate

By far the biggest mistake that most entrepreneurs and artists make is to spread their attention over multiple projects. Doing this doesn't just spread out your energy and make your efforts less effective, but it also drastically waters down your returns on a potential project that is actually worthy of your time and energy. In other words, if you play the game not to lose you will never really win. You may realize some small measure of return on the project or projects that turn out to be semi-productive, but it will be miniscule in comparison to having put all of your time and energy into one thing.

Warren Buffett says that "diversification is protection against ignorance."

What he means is that the only thing you are protecting yourself against is your own lack of information. In other words, instead of educating yourself about one thing, you are trying to protect yourself against what you don't know by investing in multiple things, which is impossible. This is a type of mental laziness with which people engage in rather than to confront the fear of the unknown. It's like building a pillow fort in your bedroom because you suspect there is a boogie man in your closet. If you just get up the courage to go look in the closet you will most likely find out there is no boogie man. Another way of saying this is to do the research, learn your craft, invest in educating yourself about it, get your hands dirty working on it, and then focus every ounce of strength that you can muster to make it the absolute best it can be.

To say it differently – it's that your inability to focus on only one thing could be due to the laziness of committing to educating yourself and refining your ability to do it. This means that rather than focusing on one thing and diving in to do the hard work of mastering it, you are trying to take the easy road of hoping that one of your many projects will magically become successful by itself. This is the popular road of many would-be entrepreneurs who are not actually true entrepreneurs. They have a series of projects spread out on their desk like a portfolio of hopefulness. They give each one just enough energy to keep it alive, but nowhere near enough to make it amazing.

When you focus on only one thing you cut out all the frivolity from your life. Instead of wasting your valuable time and energy with busy work and surface level commitment you can begin to do the real work of mastery. Now you can take your life, your work, and yourself, more seriously. Now you have become an actual threat. Now you have taken a huge step towards joining the ranks of the most productive people on the planet.

In effect, I simply cannot say enough about the power of focusing on one thing only. The other end of this is the ability to stick with it and see it through to the bitter end. I say *bitter end* because most people don't have the courage, stamina, and strength to see it through to the end. It's another reason why the last mile is the least populated. It's because everyone else has gone on to work on yet another project or idea. However, the last mile is where everything that you've ever dreamed of exists. It's where all of the magic happens and the rewards of focusing upon one thing are exponential as compared to focusing upon multiple things.

Some people may be tempted to point out that Richard Branson focuses upon multiple things, so this must not be true. This couldn't be any further from the truth. He started with one thing: *Student,* the magazine. Next, in 1973, he opened Virgin Records Label. In 1979, he bought the gay night club, Heaven. Then, in 1984, he launched Atlantic Airways. Now, of course, there were steps in between all of these ventures whereupon he built up the businesses and added extra dimensions to their foundations. But, the fact remains that he was supremely excellent at focusing on one thing at a time, until it became successful enough that it could either run itself or be sold for a profit.

Thus, the Richard Branson that you see today is now riding off of his implacable ability to laser focus his attention on one thing at a time. Now all he needs to do is to give each business his lightest touch to keep it moving in the right direction. There are many other qualities that make him who he is, but for now, we simply need to dispel the illusion that he never focused on just one thing.

What holds you back from focusing on one thing? What is the reality of it? It's actually not because you don't know what you want to do with your life. It's because you fear making the wrong choice.

But what if there were no such thing as a *wrong choice*? What if you could be set free from that designation or idea for the rest of your life? My belief is that the world would immediately become a much happier place if everyone quit believing that it was possible to make a wrong choice with their creative direction.

Here's what happens: *should*. I should do this and I shouldn't do that. I should make the right choice. I'm telling you, this kind of thinking will have you sitting on the sidelines of your life for years at a time. It doesn't get anything done and gets you no closer to living your dreams. So if you are waiting for that one right direction to go in – you now have my permission to quit waiting. Pick something you love to do and run full sprint at it. The absolute worst that will happen is that you will fail. If this happens then you have just taken your first step towards joining the ranks of the most productive people on the planet who have all failed dozens, if not hundreds, of times in their quest to change the world.

If you love it, then dive into it wholeheartedly and never look back. Cut away everything that distracts you from being the very best that you can be at it. Breathe it, live it, execute it.

#2 Dedicate Yourself to Obsessively Learning About the One Thing

This particular lesson is somewhat of a paradox. This is because the world's most productive people usually dive right into the project first, and learn about it second. You could continue with a paradox within a paradox: most of them did not finish school either. In fact, Coco Chanel, Henry Ford, Ray Kroc, Mary Kay Ash, Madame C.J. Walker, Mayer Amstel Rothschild, Frank Lloyd Wright, Andrew Carnegie, and Dhirubhai Ambani never attended any schooling whatsoever, including elementary.

But the list is much larger if you include those who either dropped out of or never attended high school: Richard Branson, Thomas Edison, Li Ka Shing, Walt Disney, Cosmos Maduka, Ingvar Kamprad, Carl Lindner, Simon Cowell, Philip Green, Cornelius Vanderbilt, Asa Candler, and Milton Hershey.

Of course, if you include those who either dropped out of or never attended college then you have to include: Steve Jobs, Bill Gates, Jenny Craig, Michael Dell, Lawrence Ellison, Barry Diller, Mark Zuckerberg, Ted Turner, Ty Warner, Giorgio Armani, Rachael Ray, David Geffen, Dave Thomas, ay Van Andel, John Paul Dejoria, Kirk Kerkorian, and Ralph Lauren.

Of course, there are a hundred more that never finished college, but you get the point.

The paradox within the paradox is that these people are the most productive people in history, yet never either attended or finished college. However, despite having little or no formal education, they went on to become the most knowledgeable people in the world within their specific industries.

So what does that tell you?

If you are paying attention, it should tell you a lot!

You do not need a formal education to be successful.

You don't need anyone else's permission to be successful.

Specific knowledge is exponentially more powerful than general knowledge.

If you learn to do one thing better than anybody else you will become wildly successful.

The world's most productive people will often drop out of formal education in lieu of real world education in one specific area. They will obsessively and doggedly pursue this real world knowledge of the one thing day and night until they know more about it than anybody else in the world. However, they rarely wait until they are fully educated on the subject, preferring to learn as they go. They would much rather be in the game, getting dirty, taking it apart from the inside out and putting it back together, a thousand times a day.

So what does this mean for you? Am I asking you to drop out of college?

No, of course I'm not.

What I *am* saying is that you need to dedicate yourself to learning about your one thing day and night, obsessively, to know more about it than anyone else in the world. You should know the intricate workings of your project and be test driving it on a daily basis. You do not need to be fully educated on it to get started, but you do need to be willing to continue to learn and improve indefinitely. It's okay to dive in as long as you are willing to be okay with making mistakes and learning from them as you go. In the end, you'll never know until you take the plunge, so better to get started right now.

A day in the field is worth more than a thousand behind the books.

Virtually every single one of the world's most productive people conduct their lives this way. They dive straight into the deep end of the pool and worry about learning how to swim after they've hit the water. They are aware that the best way to learn is by doing it and so they do it, by god. However, this does not stop them from researching and learning every single little thing that they can about it. It's just that their learning curve is exponential because they learn from the inside out.

There is no better way to learn than by doing.

#3 Be the Best at the One Thing That You Possibly Can

There is a subtle but powerful difference between striving to be the best that you can possibly be vs. competing against other people to be the best in your industry. The world's most productive people understand this difference and never fall into the competitive trap. The difference is that these productive people are never competing against you or anyone else. They are competing against themselves to be the very best version of themselves that they can possibly be.

If you understand this psychology then you understand how deadly they can be in the marketplace. It's because they do not compare themselves with anyone else. They only compare themselves to the invisible entity within their mind that always represents the highest version of themselves that they can possibly imagine. It's a standard that they will never be able to live up to and, as a result, will push themselves so far beyond the other 99.9% that they remain lightyears beyond the reach of their competition.

Do you want to be deadly?

If so, then you need to begin to visualize within your mind the absolute highest image of yourself that you possibly can. This requires a certain amount of courage as you will have to get beyond your deserving or worthiness issues to be able to do this. It also means that you will only ever compete with the invisible, never the visible. The best of the best pay little attention to what their competition is up to. You may be tempted to think that I don't know what I'm talking about, but I'll remind you that I'm not referring to the mediocre 30% who live seemingly just below the top 0.1%. Innovators do not become innovators by thinking like everyone else. It never happens that way.

Rather, the true innovator is consumed with creating something so amazing that it will literally change the way that everyone else in the world does something. Not something, but one thing.

You must be bold my friend, very bold indeed if you want to change the world. Of course, changing the world needn't be your goal. Your only goal needs to be to do the absolute best job that you can possibly do to create the absolute best product that you possibly can. In turn this means that the only standard that matters is between you and the heavens. This is the invisible standard with which the best of the best have attempted to compete with and compare themselves to throughout time immemorial.

The only way that you will be considered the absolute best at what you do is by way of insane focus and obsessive dedication to one thing. If you think about it then you will realize that all of the most productive people on the planet are known for one thing. It's true that, quite often, they have achieved other, lesser known goals. However, they are all generally known for being the very best at one thing. This is not a coincidence. This is a naturally occurring law of the Universe.

This law states: focus on one thing to the exclusion of all else and give it every fiber of your being and the Universe will come knocking at your door.

Do you hear the knock?

Lesson 2: Integration

1. Decide upon one thing that you want to be the very best in the world at and execute it. There is no wrong decision. The only requisite is that you really enjoy doing it. That's all you needs to do and then never deviate.

2. You need to obsessively educate, train, and work at being the very best you can possibly be at your craft. It's okay if you don't know much about it in the beginning, but at the end, you need to be the best in the world.

3. You can never learn too much, experiment too much, or spend too much time refining your craft. There is no such thing as "too much" when it comes to making it the absolute best you possibly can. This lesson is often what separates the one from the millions. You make it the best it can be by making yourself the best you can be. You do this by comparing yourself against the highest possible vision of yourself that you can muster.

Lesson 3

SELF-DISCIPLINE

"Talent is cheaper than table salt. What separates the talented individual from the successful one is a lot of hard work."

—Stephen King

The corner stone of every great invention, design, work of art, incredible feat of engineering, award winning photograph, Oscar winning film, global leader, and Fortune 500 Company is self-discipline. Self-discipline is the engine powering all of the absolute greatest innovations the world has ever seen. Without self-discipline we would not have roads, cars, banks, poultry, produce, homes, or apps. Without self-discipline we would still be living in the dark ages, the very, very dark ages.

Yet, the most productive people on the planet don't think of themselves as self-disciplined. Their drive and ambition simply make it impossible to not always be striving towards greatness and working on their passion. What this means is that most of the things that take us a certain amount of gumption to get going are simply a given for them.

- It is a given that they are up at 5am and put in a set number of hours every single day working on their one thing.

- It is a given that they need to keep their physical bodies in top condition to handle the extreme lifestyle of continuous dedication.

- It is a given that they do not go out and party when everyone else is.

- It is a given that they're so focused that the people around them refer to them as obsessive. This usually happens right up until the moment that their breakthrough occurs, and then everyone in the entire world suddenly knows who they are.

- It is a given that they will miss out on a lot of the fun stuff that other people do on a daily basis. It's only sacrifice if you would rather be doing it instead of following your passion, which is why they often feel as if they haven't sacrificed a single thing.

RULES OF DISCIPLINE

#1 Show Up and Do the work

In your day-to-day life you may feel as if there are dozens of things that you need to accomplish. You need to run to the bank, you need to get to the grocery store, you need to do your laundry, you need to clean your house, you need to prepare dinner, you need to check emails, you need to check Facebook, and you need to feed the cats. Yes, there are dozens of items that vie for your attention every single day. This doesn't make you special though because every single person on the planet has this same list of things to do, every single day. Sure, some folks have an extended list of items that need to get checked off. But, ultimately, we all have a lot to do on a daily basis.

With so many things to do every day it becomes difficult to discern the things that are actually important vs. the things that are a waste of your time and energy.

Here is a question for you: *have you done anything today that is going to change the quality of your life 5 years from now?*

Most likely the answer is "no." The reason is because, if you are like most people, then you pack your daily schedule with busy, neurotic, incessant "need to dos" that merely keep you feeling productive. However, these items rarely move you forward in life. Usually, they are merely assignments that you give yourself to stay busy. They also serve a lesser known, more insidious purpose: they keep you living the same life over and over again. This type of life has a name: *the comfort zone.*

Another way of saying this is that these items have become your excuse for not living the life of your dreams. *Sound harsh?* Which sounds harsher: doing busy work for the next 40 years, living the same life over and over again, every single day? Or, getting your priorities straight and, as a result, ultimately living the life you've always dreamed of?

Busy work never led anyone to their fortunes. It does lead to the temporary feeling of accomplishment. Of course, if you think about it, this is very similar to an addiction to crystal meth. You feel great for a minute, but then you need to come back for more. In the meantime, the quality of your life does not improve; in fact, it gets worse. It's kind of a harsh analogy, but it's much closer to the truth than you realize. The addiction to busy work is usually due to the underlying feeling of not moving forward in your life. This is because you have not decided to execute on your dreams.

People find all kinds of reasons not to show up and do the work.

One of the things I used to see in the gym over and over again is what I refer to as "the special technique syndrome." Having been a dedicated gym rat my entire life, I've witnessed just about every single thing that you can possibly see take place inside of a gym. One of the repetitive behavioral patterns I observed over time would generally occur when a brand new member signed up at the gym. I noticed the propensity of a certain percentage of new members to utilize some sort of awkward or unorthodox technique to perform a basic exercise. Instead of doing the exercise the way it was designed to be performed the individual in question would use some sort of specialized twist on the form.

So the question is: *why would one do this?* Were they aware of some sort of magical secret that all of the fitness professionals and workout veterans were not? Were these brand new members, one after another, about to revolutionize the fitness industry with an all new, never before seen set of exercises? The answer = no. The only reason that you would use some sort of awkward, specialized form on an exercise is if you were hoping for quicker results.

The thing is: there is no such thing as "quicker results" in the gym. It's real simple. You show up and do the work. Period. Then, the next day, you show up and do the work again. Repeat that for 30,000 days and you are good to go.

While watching these folks and their special techniques I was able to make an incredibly accurate prediction on a consistent basis. The prediction was this: the more specialized and varied their techniques and workouts were, the less likely they would be to continue exercising in the gym past the one month marker.

Why?

It's because people who try to use special techniques or modifications are trying to get quicker results and are not actually interested in doing the work. Another way of saying this is: if you need to be entertained, or you need to try special techniques, then you will never achieve your goals. It's because you are not dedicated to doing the work, which is the only way to get anywhere in this world, ever.

The famous rap artist and producer Dr. Dre said that out of 27 years in record producing he had only ever been out of the recording studio for a total of two weeks. Two weeks! Now *that* is dedication.

Do you think that he ever read a magazine article on record producing, saw a shortcut, tried it out, and realized there was a quicker way to produce records?

Hell no. If you told him this he would most likely flip you off and step back into the studio to continue doing the work.

There is no busy work you need to do to prepare yourself. There is no special technique you need to master. There is no healing work you have to do on yourself.

You only need to do one thing: show up and do the work, every single day for the rest of your life. If you have to do laundry, that's fine. You can start on it after you've gotten your minimum number of hours in on your project. If you need to take the car in to get the oil changed it's totally fine. You can do that after you've gotten your minimum number of hours in on your project. If you need to clean the house and it's 8pm, sure thing; as long as you've gotten your minimum number of hours in on your project, clean away. The only real exception is if you have children. Then, they come first. Everything else, though?

Yeah, I think you get the point. The point is there is no excuse good enough to live the same life over and over again, forever. If there is, then you'll never achieve uncommon success and join the level of the most productive people on the planet.

I don't think that's what you want so it's time for you to get to work. Figure out the minimum bar for the daily number of hours you need to put in to make your dream become a reality and execute it. Then, show up and do the work, every single day. And never look back.

#2 Never Celebrate Before it's Accomplished

External validation is a real bitch. It's a bitch because it is the absolute killer of dreams. It's why most people don't get past the door on the way out into the world to achieve amazing success. External validation is the need for approval. By itself it may appear innocent enough, but it is the underlying insidiousness of the devil's work.

Think about it: how often do you feel like you've got a great idea for a project, but decide that you need to ask someone else's opinion about it first?

Every single time, right? Right.

Did you know this is the number one killer of all dreams in this world? It's the constant need to ask for external validation. It's the need for someone to give you the *okay*. It takes on many different forms though. It's often not as simple as becoming conscious of when you are about to ask someone whether they think your idea is worthy or not. That's easy. The hard part is to identify when you are seeking external validation through other means.

The one I have in mind is when you need others to recognize

that you are special. If you allow yourself to think that you are special then you will need recognition for sitting down to do the work. You will need attention and validation for doing what the world's most productive do without a single nanosecond's hesitation.

And what is one of the best ways to acquire attention and validation that indicate you are special? The celebration!

I've seen it happen many times over the years and as soon as I do I know this person will never achieve their dreams. Yes, harsh. But also, yes true.

If you need to celebrate, either right out of the gate or at every single milestone, then you are doomed. There is only one appropriate time to celebrate and that is when the project has reached completion. Then, by all means, celebrate away. This is your time to celebrate the hard work, dedication, discipline, and drive that got you through it all. This is your time to take note that you have begun to take yourself seriously.

Is it time to stop? Is it time to retire? Hell no. You are just beginning. In fact, it's possible that you've barely gotten your feet wet.

Consider Soichiro Honda, the founder of the Japanese automotive company, Honda. It's one of the most epic, prolific, and archetypical success stories of all time. Here is a man who never got a break from anyone, ever. He worked his entire lifetime experiencing setback after setback. He only ever received criticism for his work from his peers. He was born in 1906 and did not realize any level of success until 1949. When he was finally at the finish line and his Honda factory looked as if it would succeed, it was badly bombed during World War II.

He had already gone through every imaginable level of hell, including getting kicked out of Toyota, being divorced by his wife because he sold her jewelry to finance the business, almost dying from a car wreck during a race, and now after everything else his factory was bombed. *Did that stop him?* No. Despite the fact that there were massive gas shortages and their country was under attack, he continued to innovate ways to carry on his life's mission.

Due to the severe gas shortages in Japan he decided to build himself a motorized bicycle to save money by conserving gasoline. Other people saw his invention and wanted one for themselves, so he built several more and people loved them. They became an immediate hit. He then decided to call every single bicycle shop in the entire nation, which was several thousand, and see if they would invest in his product. Many of them agreed, but there was not enough metal to build all of the motorized bicycles. *Did that stop him?* No. He went out and collected all of the metal from the bombs that had been dropped on Japan during the war. From this he was able to begin mass production of the first ever motorized bicycle, and the rest is history.

The point is this: did he ever consider himself to be special for all the dedication, hard work, and sacrifices that he made? No. Did he ever stop and celebrate that he had done it or arrived? No. He continued doing the work and never stopped to celebrate until Honda was an actual company making a profit.

Stephen Pressfield, the author of *Bagger Vance*, tells the story of when he finally finished the very first manuscript of his first novel. After years and years of struggle and toil, he had finally done it. He was so excited that he wanted to tell someone about it and who better than the man who had inspired him to finally finish what he started. Pressfield, describing the incident: "I trotted down the street to my friend and mentor Paul Rink and told him the triumphant news. 'Good for you,' he said without looking up. 'Start the next one tomorrow.'"

Starting to get the point? You aren't special because you finally decided to get to work, so you don't need a celebration.

In fact, there is an inverse algorithm that deals specifically with the relationship between feeling special and achieving goals.

$$\frac{\text{The more special}}{\text{you think you are}} = \frac{\text{the less likelihood that you}}{\text{will achieve your goals.}}$$

If I knew math better I would have made a clever equation to additionally indicate the growing likelihood of never accomplishing anything meaningful that directly corresponds to the increased emotional need of feeling special. It's a real shame that so many dreams are destroyed by that word. Parents with the best of intentions set their child up for a lifetime of struggle by telling him how special he is. Unfortunately, you are only setting your child up for a life of mediocrity, at best. At worst, you are setting him up for a never-ending emotional roller coaster from hell.

The problem is that when you think you're special you need credit for everything that you do. You need attention, validation, money, or credit for doing the most mundane things. This means that you need a reward, the celebration.

Guess what? You aren't special, not even close. You could very well be a badass who is going to follow the lessons in this book straight into the highest caliber of fame and fortune possible on the planet. But, you aren't special.

And since you're not special you don't need a celebration to do it. Just do it. You may not like me right now, but by god, you'll thank me later!

#3 Adhere to a Daily Routine

All of the most productive people on the planet have a daily routine which they execute every single day. They already know what they are going to do the next day before they even wake up. They have a set routine that centers and grounds them and holds them accountable to being the very best that they can possibly be. They have a certain amount of exercise, a certain form of meditation, a certain type of diet, and a certain length of reading or research that they do every day. They also have set times for when they go to bed, when they get out of bed, when they meditate, when they exercise, when they have meetings, when they work on their project, and when it's time to quit working for the day.

They begin their day, every day, in the exact same way. And they end their day, every day, in the exact same way.

You think it's boring? To get bored by your daily routine is to allow resistance to enter into your life. Remember, if you need to be entertained, then you'll never make it.

I'm not talking about enjoying the arts, watching a movie, spending time with your family, or taking vacations to exotic locations. These activities are all valid. But, they are not part of your daily routine or that of the most productive people on the planet either. These activities are for after you're done with your daily schedule or after you've finished your project.

Your daily routine is your lifeline to gaining momentum in your life.

This means that every day you will have a set time for when you wake up and a set time for when you go to bed and you will never deviate. You will have a set meal plan and will already know what you are going to eat. You'll have a set amount of time for meditation and visualization. You'll have a set time for when you start working on your project. You'll have a set time for when you stop working on your project. You'll have a set time for when you exercise.

You will leave nothing to chance. You are taking full control of your life and your destiny and leaving nothing in the hands of the gods of fate. You will ride this routine like it's an Arabian Stallion trying to outrun a 300km/second tidal wave on the beaches of Madagascar. You understand that to get off of your routine is to the demise of your dreams. It's to allow for the creation of starts and stops, ups and downs, or peaks and valleys that ultimately get you nowhere.

The daily routine keeps you emotionally balanced. When you get regular meditation and exercise on a daily basis you not only stay balanced, but you also evolve your psyche. Every hour, day, week, month, and year that you stay on your routine develops your willpower. This kind of structure is what will begin to get you ever closer, step by step, to joining the ranks of the world's most productive people.

Sylvester Stallone was known for a lot of things, but not chiefly among them was being a writer. In fact, he was a prolific writer. In fact, writing was his first calling when he was still an unknown in show business. However, he openly admitted to not being a very good writer. So how did he go on to write over two dozen different screen plays?

He had a daily routine.

Stallone woke up every morning at 4:30 so that he could be writing by 5. He would write for hours a day and sometimes it would be terrible. It didn't stop him from continuing to write though. He knew that if he could get in there, do the work, and get it done, that ultimately he would be successful.

And the results? Yes, obvious.

- Warren Buffett reads 4 hours a day, every day.

- Martha Stewart has her daily green juice blend at 7:30am every morning.

- John Grisham starts every morning at 7am with the same coffee, same desk, and exact same mindset.

- Sheryl Sandberg turns her phone off every night before bed.

- Russell Simmons meditates twice a day at the same two times every day.

- Barrack Obama wears the same basic outfit every day so as not to get distracted by what's important.

- Danica Patrick runs for one hour every single day.

- Elon Musk's day starts at 6am every day and is planned meticulously down to the minute.

- Jean Paul Dejoria wakes up every morning and takes the first 5 minutes to feel gratitude before getting out of bed, every morning.

If you want to eventually be considered among the most productive people on the planet then you will need to create a daily routine that you adhere to through thick and thin, no matter what. Once created and executed, nothing should be able to knock you off of your routine. And after you've been doing it for a year solid you will have separated yourself from millions of other wannabes who are still enduring the tough ups and downs of not having committed to a daily routine.

Lesson 3: Integration

1. Show up and do the work, every, single day. This means you work on your craft every day. There is no getting around this. You show up, you work, you go to bed, you get up, and you do it again.

2. Avoid wanting to celebrate at every single milestone along the way. It usually means that you need external validation and special treatment for your accomplishments. It also means that you'll never make it. Better to walk softly and become a billionaire then to celebrate loudly and wake up with a hangover.

3. Figure out the exact daily routine that you need to create for yourself to maintain an optimal state of creativity and productivity. Then, execute it, every day for the entire rest of your life. It may need to be adjusted occasionally when your needs change or if you discover a more optimal way of getting yourself into the desired state. But, you never quit doing it on a daily basis. The daily routine is your lifeline to maintaining an optimal state of productivity.

Lesson 4

CONTROL YOUR ENVIRONMENT

"If you stay ready, you ain't gotta get ready, and that is how I run my life."

—Will Smith

One of the essential elements to staying productive is to create the exact right environment that supports your optimal state of productivity. All of the world's most productive people have a tendency to search for and isolate the exact environmental circumstances which will promote their ability to stay creative. Since it can be difficult enough to get your creative juices going in the first place, it makes it of paramount importance to figure out how to hold onto, cultivate, and stretch this state out so that you can milk it for all it's worth.

Once you get your creative energy going the last thing you want is to get knocked out of that state by unwanted distractions. You need to make sure that you have an environment where you will not be interrupted by anyone or distracted by anything in the physical area itself, but which simultaneously inspires you to get into a creative state of mind. It's not as easy as it sounds. However, once you establish the right environment, then it will be much easier for you to do your work on a consistent basis.

Many years ago I entered the home of a famous Hollywood Producer as a guest of a friend. I didn't know him and do not have permission to reveal his name. However, what I will never forget is his workroom. It was a room that was separated from the rest of the house with a window overlooking the valley. The desk was big and made of polished oak. The chair was wood also, made apparently of the same oak. The room had a high arch ceiling and there were huge bookcases lining the walls, on either side of the desk, full of books. The desk itself was clear except for the laptop computer sitting on it. There were also built in surround sound speakers throughout the room. There were no paintings or images on the walls to distract from the sole focus of the room: which was to create.

It was perfect and I was transformed.

From that day forward I was aware that one of the characteristics which separate out the world's most productive people from all the rest was the prioritization of the perfect environment. It simply wasn't a coincidence that he could produce movie after movie and have millions of people watch each one. It all had to do with this room. I could feel the energy of it, vibrating and pulsing. It said to me, "Spend time here each day and you will create new worlds."

RULES OF ENVIRONMENT

#1 Never Have Anyone in Your Circle Who Doesn't Hold You to the Highest

An infamous Madonna quote is, "I'm tough, ambitious, and I know what I want. If that makes me a bitch, okay." She was referring to her outspokenness and ambition at the time she said it. However, she was also referring to something else. She never tolerated people who didn't hold her to the highest to stay within her sphere of influence. She never spent a New York minute with anyone whom she felt had an ulterior motive, judged her for being who she was, or tried to control her in any way. Part of her ability to stay in an ultra-productive state was that she never listened to anyone about anything, ever. In turn, this freed her mind up to maintain a highly productive state that has spanned for more than three decades.

In order to become ultra productive you may very well have to eliminate some of the people from within your inner circle. You simply cannot have people within your environment who do not hold you to the absolute highest if you wish to one day be considered as one of the most productive people on the planet. This is because the average person will do and say things that will distract you from your mission or objective. You can't have someone who is asking you questions about what you are working on or giving you their unsolicited advice. You can't have someone telling you what to do or what not to do.

- You can't have someone sitting next to you firing up a bowl while you are trying to write your manuscript.

- You can't have someone trying to convince you to go out for a beer while you are putting together your business plan.

- You can't have someone listening to death metal while you are trying to sing the lyrics to your new song.

- You can't have someone telling you how awesome you look when you have barely worked out for one week.

- You can't have someone telling you to get a job when you know in your heart that you are on the right path.

- You can't have someone trying to convince you to do anything other than the work when you are trying to focus on doing the work. Period.

Your first order of business is to take full, strong, and ultimate control over who you allow into your circle of influence. We'll cover this rule in more detail during the next lesson, but for now your job is to start cutting. Realize that, for the world's most productive, not many make the draft cut to remain within their sphere of influence. This is not about being a mean person. It's about doing what it takes to make the greatest contribution to humanity that you possibly can.

#2 Create the External Circumstances Under Which You Work Best

The world's most productive take absolute control over their environment and don't leave a single element to chance. Their entire day is structured around an environment that keeps them in an ultra-productive state. They do not allow anything, whatsoever, to get in under the radar and enter into their sphere of influence that could potentially disrupt that state. That option just doesn't exist. Another way of saying it is that their entire day is preplanned and designed to exact specifications.

They know exactly how they want to wake up in the morning.

Some of them spend a purposeful amount of time in bed feeling gratitude. Some of them meditate for 20 minutes. Some of them immediately put on their sweats and take a jog. Some of them put on their coffee and read the paper. Some of them take their dogs for a walk. But, whatever it is, they already know exactly how they want it to go down and you can believe that it happens that way, every single time.

They know exactly what kind of environment they want to work in.

Some of them like to be alone in their workroom with classical music. Some of them like to meet with their team at exactly 9am every morning. Some of them answer several hundred emails in their office while sitting in silence. Some of them prefer their private studies. Some of them like to sit in a café surrounded by botanical gardens. Some of them like the energy of the New York office corner suite. Some of them take conference calls while sitting in the backseat being flown or driven to their next location. Some of them only take conference calls at one time of day and only for one hour. Some of them are on the phone all day long. They each have a slightly different optimal work environment, but they all create that exact same work environment, every single day.

In order for you to create the exact right environment, one that supports your optimal state of productivity by keeping you in a creative state of mind, you may need to experiment a little bit. It didn't happen for me by chance: I had to use trial and error to discover what was optimal for me. I eventually discovered that I worked best at a certain time of day, in a certain physical environment, and with a certain type of music. However, once I figured out what key elements needed to be in place within my work environment, I never deviated, not once.

Once you have experimented long enough to discover what works for you then you need to stick with it. You need to figure out a way to recreate that exact same environment every single day. It's like the Gold prospector who finally finds a vein of gold in the mountains after a decade of fruitless excavation. Why in the hell would he continue to prospect if he finally found a vein of gold? I think we can all agree that would be absolute lunacy. Figuring out the exact right environmental factors that get you into an ultra-creative state is like finding your own vein of gold. Once you find it then you need to stay on it and continue to mine it.

In the same way, once you discover the environmental factors that get your creative engines going, it's your job to make that a daily habit. This is an absolutely essential piece of the puzzle if you want to achieve the level of success that puts your name in the history books. Find your creative haven and then replicate the environment that supports it on a daily basis. This leaves nothing to chance and precludes the possibility of needless starts and stops. Your golden ticket lays in the creation of momentum, and you accomplish this through the seamless replication of the perfect environment.

#3 Keep Both Your Home and Your Work Environment Organized

People continue to debate over the efficacies of keeping your home and work environment clean. I'm not overly concerned as to the differing opinions around some of the geniuses of our time concerning their cleanliness or lack thereof. The truth is the truth is the truth: to achieve uncommon success means to take on uncommon responsibility. The only way to handle that level of responsibility is to be incredibly structured. The only way to maintain that level of structure is to have an organized home and work environment.

Remember, we are not talking about the top 30% in this book. We're discussing what it takes to break into the level of the most productive people on the planet which is represented by the 0.1% bracket. If you are shooting for anything less than that, then yes, you can get away with a cluttered desk or an unkempt bedroom. But if you are still reading this book then I will take it for granted that you have the desire to become someone who is considered as world class caliber.

I'll say it again: this is a different level of the game. It is uncommon. It's a level of the game of which, upon the actualization of success of the individual, the average person will attribute to luck, chance, connections, or being in the right place at the right time. Of course, these are all excuses to feel better about not pursuing your own dreams and aspirations. When you get down to it, it has nothing at all to do with luck. It has more to do with an insane drive, work ethic, dedication, and a level of organization that defies rational explanation.

If you consider your home as your sacred sanctuary of rest and rejuvenation, then you should consider your work space as your sacred temple of creativity.

You honor both of them by keeping them completely organized at all times. It is said that your work and home environments represent what's happening within your subconscious mind. If your home or work is cluttered then you have unconscious clutter in your subconscious. Conversely, if they are clean and organized, then you have less unconscious debris floating around within your subconscious.

You may be tempted to say: well, just because you have a clean work environment doesn't mean that it automatically clears up your subconscious mind. Of course it doesn't. What it does do is develop willpower and make you mentally stronger. It will also help you to highlight any lagging areas in your mind that you are unconscious of. In other words, if you do keep your work space clean and organized, then any issue within your subconscious will be easier to spot. Once an issue is highlighted it means two things: first, it is less easily able to sabotage you. To get sabotaged means to get caught off guard. Second, it means that you can begin to focus on this issue and integrate it. Ultimately it means there will be less to distract you from what is really happening inside of your mind. The more you dot I's and cross T's the less your subconscious sabotage mechanisms will be able snag you up and keep you from doing the work.

In fact, you could argue this to be the biggest benefit of

keeping your home and work environments completely organized. It will keep you mentally clear and enhance your ability to execute important decisions on demand. It will also keep you in a powerful state of productivity because it enables you to focus on the most important thing: your work.

Lesson 4: Integration

1. Never allow interlopers to take up space in your life. In this instance, an interloper is someone who doesn't hold you in the highest possible regards by honoring who you want to become. Punt. Next.

2. Create the exact right environment in order to elicit and maintain your optimal state of creativity. This means that you need to discover the physical surroundings, sounds, and times of day that work best for you. Once you have created the exact right environment then you need to protect it at all costs. This is your sacred space.

3. Keep your home and your work places organized. Do not allow papers and things to build up and begin to clutter either environment. This means that you are becoming unconscious. When this happens you will have compromised your ability to stay productive. Instead, stay organized, always.

Lesson 5

BOUNDARIES

"It takes a great deal of bravery to stand up to our enemies, but just as much to stand up to our friends."

—J.K. Rowling

Disciplining yourself to take all of the necessary steps to propel you to the heights of uncommon success is not easy. It takes developing an iron clad willpower and staunch determination to see it through to the very end. One of the things that you don't need to have is anyone around you who is either consciously or unconsciously trying to undermine you. This is one of the lessons that all of the most productive people on the planet have had to learn the hard way.

You can't set sail with the anchor down.

No matter how hard you try you simply cannot change people. You may think that they'll get on the same page with you mentally and begin to make the necessary changes within their own lives. You may hope that your discipline and determination will rub off on them. And you may be hoping for a very long time.

It's a difficult but necessary lesson to learn if you want to one day be considered as one of the best of the best in the world at what you do. It's the lesson of learning to create boundaries. What makes it so hard is the risk of losing people who you had previously enjoyed spending time with. Yet the paradox is that if you are at risk of losing them because you want to elevate yourself in the world, then they are probably not a true friend.

I say this because true friends want the very best for you no matter what. A true friend is someone who will stand by any decision that you make in the vein of bettering yourself and achieving your goals. They would never dream of standing in the way of your dreams. The problem is that most people don't think this way and so are unable to recognize their behavior as something that would hold you back. This means that it is up to you to make this distinction and create the necessary boundaries with your friends, associates, and family members.

Even if you have been reincarnating for thousands of lifetimes, right now you only have one life to live. So, is it really worth it not to live that life in order to keep someone else emotionally comfortable? Or, for that matter, is it worth not living that life in order to keep yourself emotionally comfortable?

It's the only reason why we keep those relationships going, the ones that hold us back in life. We keep them because they're comfortable. They provide us with a certain amount of emotional comfort and they provide the other party with a certain amount of emotional comfort. But that's the rub. If you need to be emotionally comfortable then you will not make it to the top 0.1% of world class caliber achievers. Comfort is not part of this formula by any means. If anything, discomfort is a part of the equation. Learning to be comfortable with being uncomfortable is part of the journey to becoming one of the most productive people on the planet.

So get ready to break way out of your comfort zone in order to create the boundaries you need to soar to heights undreamed of.

RULES OF BOUNDARIES

#1 Never Allow Anyone to Keep You from Your Work

By now you know that a top priority is to show up and do the work every single day. To keep your creative engines going you need to show up and be present in the mechanics of your own dreams on a daily basis. There is no exception to this rule. What this means for you is that you can't have an individual in your life who is making it difficult for this to happen. You can't have a nagging spouse, needy relative, codependent friendship, or any other type of relationship that keeps you from showing up to do the work.

If you let your friend Sarah cajole you into going out for a drink on Wednesday night then Thursday morning you will be less able to do the work. And you know this because the last time you did it your work was compromised. That business plan that you had been working on turned into absolute shit when you wrote hungover. You weren't able to continue working on it until Friday morning, but even then you still weren't as mentally clear as you were at the beginning of the week. You started off the week so well and you were making real progress. Now your whole week is trashed because you allowed yourself to be convinced to go out for drinks on Wednesday night.

So whose fault is it?

Is it Sarah's? Or is yours? Well, you answer that question with another question: whose responsibility is it to run your life? Is it Sarah's? Or is it yours?

Right, you have your answer.

It's Sunday night and you are preparing for the week when your phone rings. It's your nephew, Timmy. Again. And this time he doesn't just need emotional support, he needs a place to stay for a couple days. Already you're thinking about the last time that happened and how well it worked out for you. It didn't just set you back a little bit, but it actually completely brought all of your dreams to a screeching halt. He snored at night and you could hear it all the way from the living room. He left the bathroom a mess, gross. He also left a bunch of dirty dishes in the sink. After a week went by you began to realize that he didn't actually have a "plan" per se, he was just sort of winging it. And worse, he looked as if he was getting comfortable in your living room.

So what do you do? Will poor little Timmy go homeless? Whose responsibility is it to take care of Timmy? Is it yours? Or is it Timmy's?

Right, you have your answer. Timmy will quite likely want to crash at your place every so often for a YEAR at a time because of one reason and one reason only: *he knows that he can.* You get the picture? As long as he knows that's an option, he will exercise that option.

Okay, now for the tough one: your husband John. John has been behaving morosely ever since you started working on your startup. It's true, you get home from your 9-5, say hi to the kids, help with dinner, shower, spend about 20 minutes with him and then you are out the door to your meeting. But it's getting harder and harder to ignore John's mood. He is constantly pouting, acting quiet and withdrawn, and not really supporting your vision. Sure, he says he fully supports you, but he doesn't act like it at all.

Of course, there are plenty of people who say that "he is your husband so you should be spending more time with him." But none of them have higher aspirations or dreams. At least none of them would ever dare to openly talk about or admit to having them. To do so would mean to have to admit to not feeling fulfilled, which is dangerous. It's dangerous because it implies that you need to change. This is dangerous because it means that you have to move through fear. And that's dangerous because it means that you need to get off your ass and do something.

So you're on your own. *What do you do?*

Whose responsibility is it to set things straight with John? Is it yours or is it his?

Right again, it's yours. But why is it yours and not his? Why can't he shoulder the burden for his own emotional codependency? It's because John is not like you and, in fact, not many people are. Only one in a thousand have the courage to dream big dreams and out of those only one in ten thousand have the courage to see it through to the end. This means that you are something like one in ten million. John can't be blamed for thinking like an average person since really you are the one who is different.

What does this mean for you? Yes, you got it. You need to create boundaries with John and you need to do it in such a way that he understands it's not an option. I mean, that's if you actually want to achieve your dreams. It doesn't mean that you love John any less. If anything, it simply means that you are starting to love yourself more. People who give themselves this kind of love are an invaluable commodity on the planet. They lead and inspire us to do amazing things. They almost always create lasting value that makes the world a better place.

Wait a second though, now you're asking me something else: what if this is just a hobby that I want to develop on the side? Do I really need to go all or nothing and isolate myself from everyone I care about then? Let me ask you this: is it your hobby or is it your dream? Once in a while, a rare individual comes along who is able to successfully turn their hobby into their dream. We've all heard the stories about the housewife who worked on her project part-time in between cooking meals and taking care of the kids. Now she's a millionaire. Usually, however, even then it's not true because what you find out, after the fact, is that she worked day and night, 24/7 on her *hobby*. It wasn't actually a *hobby* at all, but it was an *obsessive addiction to perfecting a craft*. Just another in a long line of illusions that need to get shattered so that you can get over yourself and get to the business of doing the work.

So we've established that it's not a hobby, but that it's your life's blood and reason for being. This means that you will have to do the tough job of setting up boundaries to protect this. It doesn't mean that you have to divorce John (I mean, I hope not), but it does mean that he will need to fully accept your mission and everything that it entails. He will need to be okay with you doing what you need to do for you. If you have to meet with your team five or six nights a week after work then that's what you need to do. If you need to spend all day Sunday going over details about the business then that's what you need to do. If it means you only spend one day a week with John then that's what you need to do.

Sometimes sacrifices need to be made in order to create the life of your dreams. Sometimes big sacrifices need to be made. However, after the initial push, usually a nice work/life balance can be established. In the beginning, though, you will definitely need to create strong boundaries around your dreams to protect them. Everyone in your circle needs to not only accept your mission, but get fully behind it. If they aren't already then it's because you haven't stepped into your power and had the appropriate conversation with them. It's ironic, but it's really "the conversation that's not up for conversation." This means that you are letting that person know, in no uncertain terms, that you will be pursuing this goal with or without them being a part of your life. Remember though, it's only an ultimatum when it's a conversation with someone who doesn't truly support your vision.

Congratulations, you have just taken a very large step in the direction of joining a very elite group of people on the planet. This is the group that makes history. They are referred to as the most productive people on the planet.

#2 Never Allow Someone to Project Their Limitation onto You

One of the things that the most productive people on the planet have been forced to do is become immune to projection. Projection is basically when you try to make your truth into somebody else's truth. Often, this is in the form of: you can do this or you can't do that or you should do this or you shouldn't do that. The world's most productive have had people telling them what they can and can't do since they were able to understand the words "you can" or "you can't." "You can't be an opera singer, but you can be a truck driver." A large percentage of the world's super achievers were people who had someone, from a very young age, projecting massive amounts of limitation onto them.

Larry Ellison had an adopted father who repeatedly told him "you are good for nothing."

Oprah Winfrey's grandmother would tell young Oprah to watch her closely when she was hanging laundry with clothespins for the people she was housekeeping for because "you will have to do this one day too."

Marilyn Monroe was told by more than one modeling agency that she "would be better off as a secretary."

Elvis Presley was told by the Concert Hall Manager of the Grand Ole Opry after he performed that night that he would be better off "returning to Memphis and driving trucks."

Albert Einstein was expelled from school and not deemed a "good learner."

Lucille Ball's drama instructors thought she was terrible and urged her to "try another profession."

Michael Jordan was cut from his high school basketball team because his coach didn't think he was "good enough."

Thomas Edison was told by his elementary school teachers that he was "too stupid to learn anything and that he should go into a field that did not require intelligence."

Charles Darwin's father would regularly tell him "you are lazy and a dreamer."

Barbara Streisand's mother told her she was "not pretty enough to be an actress" and she could never become a singer because "her voice wasn't good enough."

Walt Disney was fired from the Kansas City Star newspaper because he was told that he "lacked imagination."

The list of world class caliber people who were told they would never amount to anything when they were young is a big one. Somehow, some way, they were all able to overcome these projections and continue to believe in themselves and their dream. Even as children, these amazing beings had the faith and fortitude to never believe anything less than what was real in their own minds about themselves. They never wavered in their resolve to become who they wanted to be.

You probably don't have someone in your circle telling you that you can't do it. It's much more likely that you have people in your circle who tell you what can and can't be done. The average person believes they are helping you when they tell you to be realistic. Since they do not believe in themselves and their own abilities then they will most likely not believe in yours either.

The catch is that they may even think they want the best for you. This makes it much more difficult to discern between good advice and bad advice. It's because it could come from someone who you trust.

In fact, this could be one of the biggest problems that you will face. If you haven't developed good boundaries and a strong willpower, you will be tempted to listen to advice from the people in your circle. Since none of them are world class caliber achievers who live in the top 0.1%, it's probably not good advice. Quite simply, nobody you know thinks in the way that you need them to think in order for their advice to have any value for you. If they did then you would already be well on your way to achieving uncommon success.

Projection from a well-meaning person is almost more harmful than projection from a person who intends you ill will. As crazy as this may seem, it's better to see the wolf coming than to have it standing right next to you, whispering into your ear wearing sheep's clothing. This is because projection from people you trust gets in under the radar and has a chance to sink into your subconscious mind. Conversely, projection from someone who clearly does not have your highest interest in mind is more likely to get checked at the door.

If someone who clearly does not like you says to you, "You will never amount to anything," it may sting a bit, but it won't stick in your subconscious mind. However, if someone who you trust says, "You should really get a job and give up on your business idea, otherwise you will continue to stay broke," you'll actually consider it. Worse, you may even act on it since it's coming from someone who you believe wants the best for you. The catch is that they are not fully conscious of why they are saying what they are saying. They are actually speaking from their own subconscious limiting beliefs about life and are now projecting those limiting beliefs onto you. So in a really strange twist, you are almost better off to have your enemy tell you that "you suck," rather than to have a friend tell you to "get real."

At the worst, you'll be hurt by your enemy, but you'll get over it because you know they are your enemy. At the best, it will motivate you to prove them wrong.

At the worst, you'll actually give up your dream of running your own business when your friend says you should quit and get a job. At the best, it will bog you down with self-doubt and take you awhile to pick it back up. Effectively this means that the best outcome is that it only slows you down.

Projection is incredibly difficult to get ahold of and properly identify.

Part of the reason why you may or may not be vulnerable to projection is if you need external validation. You instantly expose yourself to projection the absolute second you feel the need to discuss your dreams or plans with your friend Jeffrey.

Now Jeffrey may or may not be into self-development or achieving goals. However, what he definitively is not is one of the world's top 0.1%. He is not a one of the most productive people on the planet. He is not Warren Buffett, Richard Branson, Oprah Winfrey, Ray Dalio, Larry Ellison, Robert Kiyosaki, Tony Robbins, J.K. Rowlings, Elon Musk, or Sylvester Stallone. In other words, unless he is a world class caliber coach that you hired to help you achieve your goals, he has no idea. What he does know really well though is average thinking and mass mind limitation.

So what did you really just do?

You opened the door to your treasure trove, your storehouse of dreams, and you let in the swine. Do you think the swine will respect your sacred temple? Probably not. It's much more likely that they'll get mud all over the kitchen floor, eat at the dining room table, and crap on the living room carpet. Don't get me wrong I love pigs, but this is a particular type of swine that you want nothing to do with. I don't mean to judge Jeffrey for being average. What I do mean to do is to direct your awareness to the effects of what asking for an average opinion will have on your ability to stay productive. It would be much better to discuss the weather or the news with Jeffrey than your dreams or goals. That is, unless you want to have to argue and rationalize with someone about why you want to do what you want to do.

Since that is incredibly draining and a total waste of your time and energy you should probably just skip it. When you share your dreams and goals with people it usually means that you aren't sure of yourself. So, get sure of yourself. Realize that no one is going to achieve your dreams and goals for you, ever. It's up to you. If you can get a grasp on that you will be less likely to succumb to the compulsive need to discuss your dreams and goals with people. In turn, there will be no foothold for the unconscious average to project their limitation onto you from.

So the next time you are getting ready to tell Jeffrey what you are up to, stop and ask yourself: *Wait, do I really need to say it, what I was just thinking about saying right now? No? I didn't, did I?*

Right. So shut up and internalize that powerful creative energy that is welling up within you and direct it towards the creation of your dreams instead. As you do, your willpower will continue to build, and a part of you that has been dormant will begin to awaken. It realizes that you might just be serious about this top 0.1% business and it has become interested.

#3 Never Let Yourself Get Drawn into Drama

The world is full of a constant, unending, incessant, neurotic stream of dramatic events. There is never a lack of something for people to gossip, complain, or argue about. It's omnipresent, at all times, everywhere you look. In fact, it's very difficult for the average person to not get drawn into it at some point throughout the day.

However, this book is not written for the average person. This book is written for you. I mean, really, if you are still reading then you are not an average person. The average person would have put this book down a long time ago because it directly counters how they think. Well, the average person doesn't actually *think* in the way that we refer to thinking in this book. They sort of exist on autopilot. And drama is part of the fuel for an individual who runs on autopilot.

Because of the fact that they do not take control of their thinking, which simultaneously means they don't access their own creativity, then drama and dramatic events become more interesting to them. We say *drama* but really we mean *pain*. Specifically, we mean *other people's pain*. This is the food for the masses, the suffering of other people. Even people who righteously argue for an end to oppression, war, greed and hunger are feeding off of the pain and suffering of other people as much as anyone else. Sometimes, more so. Note: these folks are usually not actually doing anything about it, but enjoy the drama of arguing about it.

There are all kinds of ways to get drawn into drama.

Watching the news can create an emotional state that triggers you. If you are emotionally triggered then you may begin to look for an outlet for your anger, resentment, blame, or sadness. This makes it easier for someone else to draw you into a debate or argument about it. Their trigger and your trigger hook up and you collectively create drama. Now you can also rationalize feeling triggered because you have a target to engage with and vent your emotional pain onto. It can range anywhere from an irritating debate all the way to an enraged screaming match.

The question is: *how does this help you?*

The answer is: *it absolutely does not help you or anyone else in any kind of productive way whatsoever.*

What about when your friend Jennifer who has an asshole boyfriend? Shouldn't you jump in and tell her what a jackass he is? Shouldn't you convince her to leave him? Shouldn't you be there for her when she needs a shoulder to cry on? Shouldn't you be the emotional rock for her while she tries to work it out?

The answer is: unless you want to become a counselor or a therapist, no.

Here is the problem: it's not up to you whether or not she is going to leave him or not. It's not up to you whether or not she will decide that she is worthy of better. It's not up to you whether or not she is ready to take responsibility for her own life. Since you cannot control her, nor would you want that responsibility, your best bet is to let her live her own life. It's one thing to tell someone what you see happening if they ask you; it's quite another to enable someone to carry on with their codependent behavior by always being there for them when they need it.

Of course, the larger problem is that every time you make yourself part of the drama, you set yourself back in life. Every. Single. Time. You may not like to hear this but, if your goal is to join the level of the world's most productive, then you need to heed my words. You will never, ever get there if you are too busy meddling in other people's lives.

Then there are office politics. As much fun as it may seem to get caught up in the gossip at work, the absolute second that you do, you have relegated yourself to average. Average people enjoy office politics and gossip at work. Above average people avoid it like the plague. And super achievers are only there for the paycheck or to learn a skill to be able to one day run their own business. They are definitely not there to get caught up in the drama of the latest gossip or rumors.

If you are working a 9-5 while taking the steps to build an amazing life for yourself then you are among many. There is nothing at all wrong with this. The problem isn't working at a 9-5. The problem is when you begin to define yourself by it. The more you define yourself by your job then the more likely you are to get drawn into any sort of political wars, gossip, or drama. If you are who I think you are then it's not your place to be concerned with such things.

Who cares if Terry is getting picked on by Brooke? If everyone continues to feel sorry for Terry and come to her aid, she will never learn to stand up for herself. She will never learn to create boundaries. In fact, if she leaves this job and finds another one, guess what? She will take that lesson with her and recreate a new "Brooke" in her next job.

Who cares if Fred is sleeping with the entire HR department? Let him sleep his way right into middle management. Why should you even begin to care about that? Just avoid him and you'll be fine. It's not your business.

Is your boss a jackass? Whose isn't? It's why you are reading this book, because you don't want to have to work for jackasses anymore. The more quickly you get the lessons in this book the more quickly you can quit that job and get out from under him.

Your mission is to avoid drama at all costs. Let other people be the ones who slow down to look at the accident on the side of the road. Let other people be the ones to go through relationship hell and waste a huge chunk of their lives in the process. Let other people bicker, argue, and foam at the mouth about current events. Let other people get caught up in the political intrigue at work and gossip endlessly about it over lunch break. This is not you, not now, not ever.

You need to become immune to the hook for drama and stay focused on the bigger picture. The bigger picture is you showing up, doing the work, and staying focused on what it takes to create a life that no one around you could ever possibly conceive of.

This is your destiny.

Lesson 5: Integration

1. Never allow anyone to have the power to keep you from doing the work. There is no one in the world that is important enough to keep you from pursing your goals. This means that anyone in your inner circle should respect you enough to allow you to do your work. If they don't, then it means that you have not stepped up to the plate to create the proper boundaries. Do so now.

2. Projection is when someone else attempts to make their truth into your truth, or vice versa. Your job is to never, ever accept someone else's idea of limitation. This means that you need to be solid in who you are and what you are about. You no longer need anyone else's opinion about your dreams and goals. You need to develop your will power and never allow anyone else's idea of limitation to penetrate into your subconscious mind.

3. Drama is an excuse not to show up and do the work. It's another form of resistance to doing what you need to do. If you allow yourself to get caught up in other people's drama then you will never create the space or cultivate the mental energy to work at becoming a world caliber success. It is impossible. Avoid drama at all costs. This may also mean eliminating dramatic people from your circle as well. If so, then execute.

Lesson 6

FOCUS ON THE SOLUTION, NOT THE PROBLEM

"Once you replace negative thoughts with positive ones, you'll start having positive results."

—Willie Nelson

One of the common traits and characteristics of the world's most productive is the amazing and maddening ability to always focus their attention on the solution instead of the problem. The reason it's slightly maddening is that it also has a tendency to make them into incessantly positive people. It's quite difficult to find any of them ever worried or concerned about anything. They may lose money, they may have a project that flops, and they may have a crisis develop in their personal life. However, even then, ultimately they are still able to consistently do something that most people have real trouble with. They are able to focus upon the solution instead of the problem.

In fact, the problem is treated as a given and immediately dismissed. It barely gets any air time at all. It's like there is this gear in minds of these amazing beings that, upon identification and observation of a problem, immediately shifts them into a solution-oriented state of consciousness. You just can't get them to worry about the problem. They seem to somehow inherently be aware of the fact that to worry about it is to waste emotional energy on it. To worry about the problem is almost as if to validate the problem.

"I am worrying about you so you must be important."

Negative. It's just not going to happen for these ones. Instead, they instantaneously gearshift into a creative state of solution-oriented, brainstorming madness. They will not stop until they have come up with the idea that will solve the problem. Another way of saying this is that they are aware that the same level of thinking that created the problem cannot solve it. So they shift into a higher level of thinking to create the solution instead.

If there was a dam that sprang a leak, sure they would probably attempt to repair the leak. However, for this caliber of world level achievers, they would not be satisfied with simply repairing the leak. They would not even be satisfied with designing a new dam. They would be more likely to engineer a new way to distribute water pressure more evenly so there was less pressure on the dam wall. Likely they would innovate a new method of cultivating energy with water that made the dam, itself, obsolete.

I'm not saying this has happened yet. I'm saying this is the way they think. They never focus on the problem because to do so is to think in linear terms. Instead, they focus exclusively on the solution, which is to think in nonlinear terms.

RULES OF THE SOLUTION

#1 Never Complain About the Woes of the world

At almost any point throughout the day you could describe your state of mind in either one of two ways: productive or unproductive. This book is about how to get your mind in the most ultra-productive state possible and still remain human. However, you also need to be aware of states of mind that do not serve your highest interest or help you to achieve your goals. Chief among these is the state of complaining about things that are wrong with the world.

You've seen him, right? The guy who carries on about all of the things that are wrong with the planet. Of course you have, we all have. We all know someone who enjoys complaining about all of the terrible things happening in the world.

Are there actually terrible things happening on the planet? Yes, of course there are! We're all aware of it. It's the byproduct of living in duality. And when you complain about it, how much effect does it have? How much change is brought about through mass complaining about things that are wrong with the world?

Zero.

So what's the answer? The answer is that, just because there are things wrong on the planet, does not mean that you have to define your existence in this manner. When you complain about all of the things wrong with the world it does two things: first, it contracts your thinking and ability to problem-solve. It's not a creative state of mind, but rather one of constriction and limitation. It actually begins to affect your neural network and limit your ability to problem-solve. Second, it only contributes to the mass belief in limitation. This means that, instead of actually doing something to make the world a better place, you are actively contributing to the mass belief that the world is not fair and just. You are contributing to the belief that people are helpless to create change. In effect, you have become the problem.

Here is a question for you: when was the last time you witnessed Michael Jordan complain about missing a shot? How about Jeff Bezos? Ever see him complain? Michelle Mone, what about her? Does Warren Buffett, T. Harv Eker, J.K. Rowling, Will Smith, Martha Stewart, Elon Musk, or Tony Robbins ever complain about anything? Hell no they don't.

So why don't the most productive people on the planet ever complain about anything? It's because they have all recognized long, long ago that to complain about something is to admit that you are powerless to change it. They figured out at an early age that to engage in the act of complaining means that you are not willing to be accountable, make the necessary changes, and do the work no one else is willing to do. It's easy to complain, but it's much more difficult to actually do something about it. The most productive people on the planet have already executed 50 action steps by the time that one complainer is done with their tirade.

When you catch yourself getting ready to complain about something, stop. Think about it. Ask yourself what good is this going to do for you or the people around you? What productive change is this going to bring? Since the answer to both of those questions is "zero" then you can stop yourself, knowing that you have just become a little more powerful and slightly more effective. It will build up over time. Every time you stop yourself from complaining you become less of a victim and more of a creator. You become less of someone who the world happens to and more of a creator who makes the world a better place. You become stronger, more powerful, and more on purpose.

You increase your willpower.

When you have arrived at the point where you can consistently catch yourself about to complain then you will have become very powerful. You will waste much less mental and emotional energy. Instead, now you can direct that energy towards the creation of your product. The less you complain about things the more creative your mind becomes. As your *complaining gear* begins to atrophy away, your *creative gear* begins to build up and become stronger. It's a tradeoff that brings you another step closer to becoming a world caliber success.

#2 Focus Your Attention Upon Creating Solutions

The most productive people on the planet are often so busy creating their own universe that they completely forget about all of the problems on the planet. They spend their time focusing on creating solutions while everyone else is focused on the problems. To say that they are solution-oriented still doesn't quite grasp the consciousness of these super achievers. Rather, it's more of a continuous state of creativity that holds these beings to a continual course of action. Their consciousness is so exclusively focused on the act of creating that it's almost as if they don't have any problems. What we don't see is the state of grace that's created by the state of mind they embody.

Imagine for a second that you are Richard Branson and at any given moment you are overseeing anywhere from 100-400 different companies. Do you think there aren't any problems? You would be crazy to think that, right? Right. *So what's the secret?* Why isn't Brave Sir Richard ever worried about problems? It's because his consciousness is solution-oriented, which means that he is in a constant state of creativity. It simply does not occur to him that it can't be done. When someone presents a problem he is immediately thinking "solution." He is not thinking, "Uh oh, there is a problem, what do we do now?" He knows there is always a solution and it is simply a matter of creating it. It is a matter of pulling it out of the ethers and making it manifest as a physical reality. And he does it every single day.

Richard Branson is an easy example to use because his life has been made so public and he rarely shies away from the spotlight. What we don't see is how every single one of the world's most productive people operates in this exact same manner. Whether it is Madonna tirelessly going over and over every single move in the dance routine until it is exactly right in every single performance, Elon Musk responding to every single mechanical or engineering issue with SpaceX, or when Debbi Fields was managing over 650 franchise locations around the world, we don't get to witness the state of grace they embody as they continuously brainstorm solutions to problems on the spot.

What these super achievers realize is that true happiness comes from moving through resistance and challenging yourself to grow in every conceivable way. In order to do this you have to become solution-oriented, which will enable you to view challenges as a means to expand yourself rather than as something to worry about. This is one of the great secrets to success: stay in a continual state of expansion by cultivating a creative mindset that is always seeking solutions.

Here is a question for you: when was the last time you saw an incredibly successful person complain about something? The temptation would be to think they don't have anything to complain about because they are so successful. Of course, we know this is just not true. If you think about it then you will begin to realize that you've never actually witnessed it happening. Again, I qualify this with ultra successful people, which means they are probably at least multimillionaires. I'm not talking about your thrifty neighbor who owns three condominiums and still insists on doing all the maintenance work himself. He may complain to you about the backbreaking work of maintaining these pesky condos every time you see him. He is not ultra successful nor within any sort of remote distance to the type of success and caliber that we're discussing in this book. This is also why you need to be careful who you spend time with in close physical proximity.

You could accidentally be thinking that you're receiving good advice from someone who is merely a good saver or thrifty. Does this mean there's anything wrong with being conservative with your money? No, of course not, this is how a good number of people have become somewhat successful. One might even attempt to argue that it's how Warren Buffett became so successful. There is only about a ten billion light year difference between your thrifty neighbor and Warren Buffett though. Your thrifty neighbor complains about taxes, complains about maintenance, and complains about the government. Warren Buffett does none of the above. He is always focused upon the solution and he never wavers from that. Has he had challenges or made mistakes? Of course he has, but he learns from them and moves on, quickly refocusing himself on the solution.

To achieve uncommon success and join the elite ranks of the most productive people on the planet you will need to distance yourself from any chronic complainers. That kind of energy is infective and will bring you right down with them. It's worse if the person in question has achieved some measure of success. This is what we call a "false positive," which means that if you follow their advice you are getting a faulty road map. It's possible that it will eventually lead you to some sort of achievement, but never to uncommon success, never to the elite level.

There is nothing wrong with being conservative and being

a saver as long as you are not doing it out of fear. Doing it out of practicality is doing it because it's a solution. When you do it out of fear it means that you are playing not to lose instead of playing to win.

Going back to Warren Buffett you can observe that he has always been rather conservative. Where people get mixed up about him is when they think that he plays the stock market not to lose. He actually plays the stock market to win. Here is the difference: people who spread their portfolio across several different stock investments are usually doing so because they fear losing. They fear putting all of their eggs in one basket. What they are doing is playing not to lose. They also do this because they have not put in the time and energy to research the companies they are investing in. In other words, they are making a hedge against their own ignorance. On the other hand, Warren Buffett will only ever invest in one company at a time, and only when he feels as if he knows the company intimately. So while the masses have their meager funds spread over several investments and usually through some form of portfolio manager, Warren has his funds tightly compressed into only a handful of companies which he has handpicked himself, one at a time.

This means that, while everyone else is complaining about the ups and downs of the stock market, Warren is relaxing and reading a book. He is learning something new while basking in the confidence of knowing that he has picked the very best company that he could. He is always focused on the solution and never the problem.

When you begin to retrain your mind to constantly look for solutions it will feel as if a light has turned on inside of your brain. The more you do this, the brighter that light gets. Just like any other muscle in the body, you'll need to work it out, every single day.

#3 Understanding What You Don't Want Helps You to Understand What You Do Want

One of the things that the most productive people on the planet do is to use a negative event or set of circumstances to their advantage. If a challenge does arise or a project does fail or a situation does goes badly they don't sweat it. If anything, this event becomes a catalyst of change for them. They use it to completely and fully understand what did not work and what they do not want.

If they have an executive team member who is constantly arguing with every decision they make, and it's not constructive, then they may have to fire them. They take notes from what they learned about the event and everything that led up to it. They figure out all of the things that did not work about the relationship. They quickly decide whether it was something about the way they worked together or if it was something about the executive themselves. From here they figure out what the exact opposite would look like and then set about creating that scenario. They use this negative event to create a positive one.

Throughout the day there are dozens, perhaps hundreds of

negative things that you could potentially focus upon. There are things in traffic, things on the news, things at work, things with your kids, things with your husband or wife, things with your team, things with your business, things with your marketing, and things with your life in general that aren't necessarily positive.

What if, in any given moment, as soon as you found yourself focused upon one of these items, you were able to turn your mind around and focus upon what the polar opposite scenario would look like instead? What kind of changes would that bring about in your life? Can you imagine? The potential changes in your neural network would be radical. If you could train your brain to always focus upon the exact opposite of everything that you didn't want to experience in the world then you would enter into a completely different state of mind. It is the state of mind of the ultra-productive and it is one of their primary characteristics.

Let's experiment for a minute:

Traffic is terrible this morning.

Or:

I want to have a nice, relaxing drive to work this morning.

I can't stand my job.

Or:

This job is helping me to keep a roof over my head while I work on building my dreams.

My girlfriend makes a mess in the bathroom.

Or:

My girlfriend has a tremendous amount of responsibility because she is such an amazing achiever.

The war in Syria is a real tragedy.

Or:

There is so much innovation and creativity happening in the world right now.

I don't have any clients and I don't know where they are going to come from.

Or:

There are literally millions of people in this world who need my services. I just need to reach them.

I can't stand the way that guy is wearing his pants.

Or:

The world is such an interesting and diverse place.

I haven't sold a single album yet.

Or:

The time will come when I will be selling millions of albums.

I hate it when it's cold and rainy.

Or:

I love the seasonal changes because it keeps things fresh and new.

I don't know how I am going to overcome this obstacle.

Or:

There is always a solution to every problem.

Can you see the potential power in the ability to switch your focus from what you don't want to experience to what you do want to? This ability will open previously closed doors in your life and your business. There is no measure of how much good will come to you when you can do this on a consistent basis. Even if you already feel like you are an optimistic person this exercise will still benefit you.

The real benefits begin when you start to realize how many times throughout the day you are focused on things that you don't want to experience. Since, when you focus upon something for any length of time it begins to expand and dominate your thought process, this skill is really more valuable than gold. In a way it's like taking your mind back. Another way of saying this is that if something gets your attention, it gets your power. The rubber necks of the world are some of the most helpless people on the planet. Anything and everything gets their attention and, as a result, the focus of their minds. This means they are unable to focus the power of their minds on anything lasting or meaningful. If anything and everything gets your attention then you are basically helpless. You have become a leaf blowing in the wind. Worse, since the average person is entrained to look for negative events to entertain them, then you will be helplessly drawn to negative events, one after the other, all day long.

Instead, focusing your attention upon the opposite of what you don't want to experience will force you to take conscious control of your mind and what enters into it. This is your journey straight to the top 0.1% of ultra-productivity and freedom. If you want to join the ranks of the world's most influential people then you will need to begin to take control of your mind and your focus.

Could you imagine if Jeff Bezos became angry every time he read about a world crisis in the newspaper? Do you think Amazon would have ever been built if he had allowed himself to get distracted with all of the things happening in the world that he didn't want to experience? What if every time the stock market took a dip Warren Buffett became stressed out and anxious? Could he have ever built a net worth of several billion dollars? What would have happened if Angelina Jolie went into a deep depression every time there was a humanitarian crisis in Africa? Could she have possibly been involved in dozens and dozens of productions if she had allowed herself to dwell upon this?

The ability to keep your focus on what you really want to experience doesn't mean that you are turning a blind eye to the suffering of the world. Rather, it means that you are focused upon the world that you want to create. It's also more likely that you will eventually be in an actual position to create solutions for those who are in need. This is why, in an ironic twist, the people who solve the most problems in the world wind up being the people who focus upon them the least.

Think about it. When was the last time your bitchy neighbor, who incessantly rants about the humanitarian injustices in the world, single handedly funded a new water supply for an isolated tribe in Africa? When was the last time something good happened from you being solely focused upon something that you didn't want to experience? If you think about it, it has never happened. It's only when you were able to shift your focus onto what you actually desired to experience that the good started to flow in your life again.

Your mission, should you choose to accept it, is to begin to catch yourself when you are focusing upon something that you do not want to experience. Instead, challenge yourself to figure out a scenario that represents the polar opposite and focus upon that instead. Every time you do this it puts you another step closer to joining the ranks of the most productive people on the planet.

Lesson 6: Integration

1. Complaining is for people who are too lazy to take action. It's for people who want to try to bolster their sense of self-importance who, in real life, actually feel helpless. It is not for you, ever. Cease to complain about things and instead take actions to create solutions.

2. While everyone else is focused upon the problem, you are going to do something completely innovative: you are going to focus on the solution. From this day forward you are going to train your brain to always focus on a way to solve whatever it is. No matter what, you will not get pulled into dwelling on the problem. You now have a mental gear shift that immediately puts you in a solution-oriented state of mind.

3. When you experience something that you do not want, from now on, you will retrain your mind to immediately figure out what the exact opposite is. If you experience a situation that you don't like, what is the opposite? This is how you will operate from this day forward. The exact instant something enters into your mind that you don't like you will isolate the item. After you correctly identify what it is then you will figure out what the exact opposite would look like. This is an ongoing exercise that gets easier over time.

RATE YOUR CURRENT LIKELIHOOD OF MAKING HISTORY

How true is each of the following statements for you?

(Rate your answer from 1 – 10 with 1 being the least accurate about you and 10 being the most accurate about you)

1. It's easy for me to get my day started in the morning when I wake up.

2. My day is always planned down to the last detail.

3. I take time to meditate and clear my mind every single day.

4. My desk is always free of clutter.

5. I always get some form of physical exercise every day.

6. I always know what I'm going to eat throughout the day. There are no surprises in my daily meal planning.

7. I enjoy researching and implementing new ways of doing things to increase my effectiveness.

8. I enjoy expanding my mind and challenging my beliefs about what is really true in the world.

9. I could care less about other people's opinions of my vision.

10. I am fully open to constructive feedback from qualified professionals.

11. I don't care when my success happens, I am more dedicated to creating the best product/service/work of art/end result possible.

12. I am not interested in retirement because I am not interested in being done.

13. I want to make the planet a better place for my having been here.

14. I have a strict, daily regimen that I follow every single day.

15. I am not interested in the news, gossip, or social media.

16. I am consistent in my focus, I never waiver.

17. I am more interested in creating the vision in my mind than paying attention to the one I see with my eyes.

18. I am more interested in creating a solution than discussing the problem.

19. I am easily able to see the positive in every situation.

20. I am able to execute on tough decisions immediately.

21. The only people in my immediate circle are those who fully support my vision.

22. It's easy for me to say "no" or "no thank you." It rolls right off of my tongue.

23. I am committed to finishing what I start.

24. I only take effective action-steps that yield tangible results.

25. I build in regular, weekly downtime to make sure I stay emotionally balanced.

Add up your score of 1–10 on each of the 25 questions with the sum total being somewhere between 25-250 points. Use the following chart to rate your current likelihood of making history.

Score	% Chance Making History	Productivity Level	State Of Mind
25	0	Below average	Conscious: apathetic Unconscious: undeserving
26-75	0-1	Average	Conscious: getting by is okay Unconscious: basic survival, get a job, get food, get shelter, get a mate, procreate
76-150	1-2	Above Average	Conscious: Want more out of life Unconscious: Envious, unhappy with status quo, senses something is not right

Score	% Chance Making History	Productivity Level	State Of Mind
151-200	2-3	Achiever	Conscious: Goal oriented Unconscious: Becoming aware of unconscious behaviors/ sabotage mechanisms
201-245	3-4	Leader	Conscious: Drive to Succeed Unconscious: Open to feedback/ beginning to replace old programming through awareness

Score	% Chance Making History	Productivity Level	State Of Mind
246-250	5-15	World Class	Conscious: Driven to improve the world Unconscious: Insist on critical feedback/mind-body science to achieve integration
251+	16-25	Global Leader	Conscious: I am One with all Mankind Unconscious: Illumined/Full Awareness

What to do with your score?

First, don't panic, nobody gets 250, or even remotely close to that. If someone scored themselves at a 250 it would be because Richard Branson, Jean Paul Dejoria, Oprah Winfrey, or Bill Gates took the test. However, if you take this test, you are comparing yourself to that type of standard. I'm assuming it's not because you are mildly curious, but that you want your life to radically improve. <u>If so, here is where to start:</u>

1. **Daily regimen** – Create a routine that you follow every single day that entails: exercise, meditation, your diet, your action-steps, your education, the time allotted to your project, and your bedtime/wakeup times. Make everything you do at the exact same time, every single day.

2. **Remove** – The time you spend watching the news, surfing social media, watching Youtube videos, reading magazines, gossiping about anything.

3. **Focus** – Pick one thing, one direction, one focus and put all of your time and energy into that one thing. Be the best at one thing instead of mediocre at many. This is how you will make history.

4. **Eliminate** – Complaining or excuses, forever. It only means that you haven't decided to decide. That's actually a decision. Instead, commit to it. Commit to your excellence, to your life, and to your vision. Commit to being the absolute best that you can possibly be. If you are bored by exercise, diet, meditation, or doing the work every day, you'll never make it. Get un-bored right now of doing the work, forever.

With the successful execution of these four steps you will have already set yourself light years apart from the average person who daydreams about doing something big. With consistent execution, you will eventually rise to the top and have a shot at making history. This is your start. So get started!

Lesson 7

OPERATE FROM STILLNESS

"True intelligence operates silently. Stillness is where creativity and solutions to problems are found."

—Eckhart Tolle

One of the little known secrets of the most productive people on the planet is that they all take a certain amount of time out of each day to allow themselves to be in silence. Each of them does this in a different way though. Many of them have an actual meditation practice with which they engage in every morning and night. Some of them walk their dogs or go for a jog at 5am when everyone else is still asleep. Some of them sit in contemplation on their balcony sipping their coffee before the day starts. Some of them walk around the park first thing in the morning when the mist is still rising. Just about every single one of them possesses a solid core which they derived from spending time in stillness.

Meditation has increased in popularity due to the spiritual revolution in consciousness we are currently witnessing. More and more people are turning to meditation now that the benefits have become undeniable. However, what you may not be aware of is that many of the most productive people on the planet have been meditating since long before it became popular. The reason they meditate is because all of these super achievers are always looking for ways to increase their productivity, which also inherently means to increase their mental and emotional stability.

If you are emotionally out of balance or mentally neurotic then it is virtually impossible to handle the type of daily responsibility that entails being considered a world class caliber human being. It's not that these super beings are perfect. Rather, it's that they are well aware of their imperfections. They meditate so they can continue to evolve all of the lagging areas of their own psyche and attain mental and emotional stability. Even when you think that you're mentally in control you may not fully be aware of how emotionally imbalanced you are. The average person has a relatively un-evolved emotional body. The difference between the super achiever and the average person is not the amount of evolution of their psyche. Rather, it's the willingness to do the work to evolve it.

For many of the most productive people on the planet finding meditation was like finding the missing key to unlocking their highest potential. This is because it enabled them to bring their full power to bear and focus upon what was important. It can be incredibly time consuming and energetically draining to have to constantly keep trying to find ways to feel better. This is why meditation is so popular among the super achievers of the world, because it takes care of both your mental and emotional development in one fell swoop. It also connects you to higher levels of your own intelligence and perhaps beyond. However, if you only do it for the incredible benefits of mental and emotional stability, then you will be doing it for the same reason as virtually all of the super beings mentioned in this book.

Does it have to be meditation?

Not necessarily. Like I said before, some of these powerful beings will choose to make their meditation into a jog, hike, bicycle ride, pipe smoking session, coffee session, dog walking session, or stroll through the gardens. That said, however, the reason that more and more of them are turning to the practice of meditation is that the benefits have a tendency to be exponential as compared to a simple bicycle ride. This is because clearing your head is nowhere near as profound as transcending your thinking mind. The break from ceaseless, neurotic thinking that the act of meditation provides for you is priceless. It enables your mind to rest and for your consciousness to expand. It also gives you access to nonlinear thinking, which is where all innovation and creativity comes from.

The nonlinear domain of thinking is where the iPhone came from. It's where the Mona Lisa came from. It's where the Golden Gate Bridge came from. It's where the airplane came from. It's where the refrigerator came from. It's where the wheel came from. It's where Starbucks came from. It's where the skyscraper building came from. It's where the Sistine Chapel came from. It's where the bicycle came from. It's where the paved road came from. It's where the toothbrush came from. It's where electricity came from. It's where every great invention or idea that improved the quality of life came from. It all came from the nonlinear domain of thought and through the minds of people who could tap into it.

What the world's most productive people have discovered is that meditation helps you access this level of thought in a sustainable way, indefinitely. It's like having access to a treasure trove of innovation on demand. You only need to have the desire to set aside a certain amount of time each day to be able to access this domain. However, the average person is too addicted to their own thinking as "who I am" to be able to get over themselves long enough to engage with meditation.

When you reconnect with stillness, and are able to stop the wheels of your mind from constantly spinning, then you can begin to access levels of thought that were previously unavailable to you. You will enter the domain of the nonlinear and begin to have ideas and thoughts that have real power. Mentally trying to think your way through situations rarely creates lasting solutions. Now you will gain valuable insight into truly innovative ways, means, and methods of creating solutions, designs, and inventions that stand the test of time. The world's most productive have been doing this all along.

There is nothing new about sailing the waves of the nonlinear mind using meditation as the boat, but you could very well be new to the boat. Welcome aboard.

RULES OF STILLNESS

#1 Do Not Overthink the Situation

One of the habits you may have is the tendency to do what most people do, which is to over-mentalize everything. This means that you try to think your way through every obstacle, situation, or perceived problem. It's exhausting and not only wears you down, but usually does not create any lasting or sustainable solution to your problem. This is because of the timeless adage "the same level of thinking that created the problem can't solve the problem." You need to enter into a completely new realm of thought in order to create an actual solution. Ironically, this realm requires less thought and more stillness.

If you are constantly thinking, thinking, thinking then you will not be aware if the actual solution is presented to you. If your mind is too busy spinning because you are going crazy trying to figure it out then you will be less likely to allow actual innovation to enter into your mind. Again, this is because innovation comes from the nonlinear domain of thought, not the linear. If you are trying to think of a solution to a problem then you are engaged in linear thinking. This is not inspired thought, but is thought that is being forced through your mind to will a solution to happen. Innovation never happens this way and you are only ever going to drive yourself insane doing this. If anything, this is how anxiety and neurosis are created. If you continue to try to think your way into and out of every situation in life you will never rise above the heavy cloud of mass mind neurosis. You need a way to transcend linear thinking on a regular basis so that you can gain access to the level of thought where actual solutions exist.

When your mind is constantly working all of the time there is no room for inspiration to happen. Inspiration is when your Soul tells your mind that you are looking at something you love. The gateway to love is through the nonlinear domain. You can't think your way into loving something. You can only follow what feels right for you and this can only happen when you stop thinking for a minute. Another way of saying this is that love can only exist in the linear domain of thinking as a mentalization or a concept. In other words, it is virtually meaningless until it is felt or experienced in the nonlinear domain.

Have you ever noticed how much the most productive people on the planet, despite the fact that they all have insanely busy schedules, manage to have a lot of fun? Part of the reason for this is that they're all inherently aware that to think about the same thing for too long is to diminish your effectiveness. Warren Buffett is infamous for spending an inordinate amount of time and energy getting to know every single thing about a company that you possibly can, down to the daily habits of its CEO and Board Members. After meticulous research, observation, and inquiry, if he is satisfied he will make the purchase and invest in the company. Conversely, after it's all said and done, he won't give it another second of his time. He will spend an inordinate amount of time thinking and researching, but this will be followed by relatively long periods of inactivity.

So what is he doing and why?

First, he is acting on inspired thought. This means that he is engaging with the market and prospective buys only when he feels moved to do so. Second, he is only thinking in linear terms when he needs to do research and learn something specific. Once this is done, he returns to the nonlinear domain of thought and allows his mind to explore books and contemplate. He never spins his mind endlessly trying to figure out a solution to a problem. He is aware this is a waste of time and will diminish his effectiveness.

Albert Einstein said, "The monotony and solitude of a quiet life stimulates the creative mind." It is said that he didn't actually think up $E=MC^2$. Rather, it occurred to him during one of his quiet, contemplative moments while he was smoking his pipe.

Steve Jobs said, "That's been one of my mantras - focus and simplicity. Simple can be harder than complex; you have to work hard to get your thinking clean to make it simple."

Anthony Hopkins said, "We are dying from overthinking. We are slowly killing ourselves by thinking about everything. Think. Think. Think. You can never trust the human mind anyway. It's a death trap."

Bruce Lee said, "If you spend too much time thinking about a thing, you'll never get it done."

Usain Bolt said, "I've learned over the years that if you start thinking about the race, it stresses you out a little bit."

Zhang Xin said, "Many Chinese companies are run like military camps with military discipline (over-mentalization). We do not run a company that way. It does not help the creative process."

Charlie Chaplin said, "We think too much and feel too little."

Jonathan Safran Foer said, "I think and think and think, I've thought myself out of happiness one million times, but never once into it."

Lao Tzu said, "Stop thinking and end your problems."

It's one thing to obsess over the details of your company

or your work of art, which is typically another hallmark of the most productive people on the planet. They are definitely perfectionists in the sense of obsessing over the creation of the absolute best version of whatever they are working on before releasing it to the public. However, it's quite another thing to overthink things to the point where you have rendered yourself ineffective. The average person who tries to follow in the footsteps of the world's most productive will fall into this trap. Not fully understanding how the super achievers of the world got to where they are in life, they will attempt to think their way through parallel situations to the point of neurosis. Eventually, many will wind up on Xanax or its equivalent due to the feelings of extreme anxiety and depression this has a tendency to create.

It's ironic that the answer is actually to think less and allow more. It's not that super achievers don't think, but that their thinking is simply much more effective. When you pull a thought from the nonlinear domain you are pulling it from the very fabric of creation. Doing this increases the likelihood that you will create something so profound that it will radically enhance the quality of life for literally millions of people on the planet. It also means that your action steps are likely to be exponentially more effective as well since you will be taking inspired actions instead of meaningless actions. People who are unclear about how to proceed in their business will overthink things and then, as a result, engage with just as many meaningless action steps. Part of this has to do with some of the previous lessons mentioned in this book. Once you are clear about what you want to focus on, a lot of the frivolous actions that you've been taking will become apparent. The other part has to do with not just doing to be doing. If you are not taking inspired actions then you are not on your purpose. This is often because you are overthinking the situation.

#2 Get Quiet and Withdraw From the Workplace

Many of the greatest breakthroughs in innovation have come through moments of stillness. Have you ever noticed that when you take a vacation or go out of town for the weekend that your creative mind has a tendency to come alive? It's the strangest thing that, when you take time to get away from your work routine and allow your mind to quiet down, it will actually pick-up in activity. But, to be clear, it's not the usual activity of overthinking. Rather, this type of thought is more likely to be inspired thought. It's almost as if the cage door was lifted and your mind is set free to roam into uncharted territory.

Why is that? Why does it take getting away from your work to become more innovative?

The reason this is true for most people is because most people continue to obsess over the same things every single day. Their daily routine consists of getting up and looking at the same problem in the exact same way as the day before. In other words, their daily routine has become a neurotic grind on the gerbil wheel of hell. Of course, this is the polar opposite of how the world's most productive people operate.

The reason they don't have to get away from the grind to stay creative is for many reasons, some of which have already been covered in previous lessons. However, specifically here, the reason is due to the fact that getting away from work is built into their daily routine. When you love what you do and you love how you've built your day, then there is nothing to escape from. If every day you are building in time for yourself to be quiet, time for yourself to play, and time for yourself to be creative, then you won't have to wait for your trip to the Bahamas in order to feel inspired again.

Conversely, once you reach the level of success of the world's most productive, then you will be more likely to take lots of trips around the world that do inspire you. In the meantime, in order to continue to stimulate your creativity and innovation, it's a good idea to try to get away from or get outside of your daily work cycle. This could mean physically removing yourself from the city you live and work in. It could mean building in a camping trip once a month. It could mean taking a long walk around the park in the morning. It could mean taking road trips on the weekends. It's really anything that is strong enough to create a pattern-interrupt in your normal thought process.

What you need to understand is that the world's most productive people all, each one, have some way in which they reconnect themselves, every single day, to stillness. They all understand that it's the stillness that brings them the wealth of innovation and creativity that has gotten them to where they are in life. So your mission is to make sure that you take time out of each day to create stillness in your life and transcend the daily grind of trying to get things done. The things will always be there for you to do, no matter what. The more responsibility you take on the more things there will be to do. This is why it's so important now to establish the way in which you will reconnect with stillness on a daily basis before you get too busy from following the lessons in this book that you lose track.

This is an essential element to building the type of foundation that can support world class caliber success. If you are still reading then this means you. You are on a mission to join the ranks of the world's most productive and so you will need to follow their footsteps as they lead you into stillness.

#3 Wait for the Next Right Move

Another habit that is difficult for the average person to break is to stop doing something that isn't working. This is especially true when you've hit a wall or an obstacle in your business or art and don't know how to proceed. This is where one of the most profound quotes I've ever heard Oprah Winfrey say comes into play: "Be still and wait for the next right move." What she means is that, instead of trying to overthink the situation and become neurotic or depressed, get quiet and clear your mind. When you do this you can allow inspiration and higher intelligence to bring you a solution.

Of course, there is a radical difference between sitting on your couch and moping or going out and getting hammered at the bars vs. withdrawing from your problem and allowing your mind to stop spinning. One is feeling helpless and out of control while the other is taking total control and engaging your higher mind. When you are able to let go and temporarily release the need to know or figure it out then your own higher intelligence can begin to engage with the problem. When this happens you gain the ability to receive profound insights into your obstacle or situation. The resulting actions taken from this level of mind are far superior to any that you could come up with out of the neurotic frustration of trying to figure it out.

It's also important to understand the difference between waiting for the next right move and engaging in critical thinking. Sometimes you do need to engage your mind to either brainstorm or breakdown a problem into its most basic constituents. This requires that you fully engage your mind with the problem or situation to get to the bottom of it. It's also completely different from running into a wall that you just cannot seem to get around. If you have exhausted your research and looked at every possible angle and done every single thing you can do to make it work, then it could be time to step away.

It's ironic that stepping away from the obstacle will likely provide you with a solution that is 1,000 times more effective than what you would have come up with through neurotic overthinking. Again, this is because your higher intelligence, which operates through the nonlinear domain of thought, has the opportunity to become engaged with the problem. This can only happen when you force the smaller, linear thinking mind to take a back seat for a minute.

Imagine yourself sitting in the backseat of your private car being driven around by your own personal driver in New York City. You have all of these business meetings to get to, but really, there is only one meeting that is going to make you a $10,000,000.00 deal that day. As you are driving around the city you begin to realize that you're going to be late to the really important meeting. So you tell your driver to skip the other two meetings and just head straight to the really important one. But he insists on keeping your schedule and going to the first two meetings even if it means you will be late for the big one.

How frustrating would that be?!

In this analogy your driver is your linear mind and YOU represent your nonlinear mind. It may seem crazy, but this is how most people live their lives, by allowing the linear mind to take the driver's seat. Meanwhile, their nonlinear mind, which is also their higher intelligence, goes unnoticed and unheard sitting in the backseat.

This is how the average person's mind functions, if you can call it that.

The way out of this insanity is by connecting to your own higher intelligence in the nonlinear domain of thought. You do this by withdrawing your attention from the daily grind and returning your mind to stillness. You can achieve this by simply getting quiet or through the act of meditation. There are many ways to engage with stillness. You simply have to find out which one works best for you and begin to engage with it a little bit each day.

Lesson 7: Integration

1. Overthinking things is one of the biggest reasons why most people never make it to the top 0.1%. If obsessively doing the same things over and over again created amazing results then the world would be packed with billionaires. When you overthink things you burn out your mind and start to become neurotic. If you find yourself in pattern-repeat doing the same things over and over again it means you are overthinking.

2. One of the ways that the top 0.1% continue to achieve amazing results is that they will withdraw from the workplace into a space of quietude. This means that they are allowing themselves to tap into the nonlinear domain of thought which can only be accessed through stillness. Although it is not completely necessary, it is easier to access this domain of thought when you spend time each day in silence. This is why daily meditation is so powerful: it is an easily repeatable technique in which you can access the nonlinear domain of thought through stillness on a daily basis.

3. Occasionally you will authentically get stuck and not know what to do. This is okay and happens to most of the super

achievers on the planet. When this happens, get quiet and wait for the next right move. When you retreat to stillness, take a break, or go on vacation, you provide your higher mind with an opportunity to work through the problem. This means that you are more likely to be able to receive an actual solution from the nonlinear domain of thought. The solution received from this level of thought is 1,000 times more effective than something you think of through the linear mind.

Lesson 8

BE YOURSELF

"Always be yourself, express yourself, have faith in yourself, do not go out and look for a successful personality and duplicate it."

—Bruce Lee

Something that has a tendency to really trip people up on this planet is the difficulty in staying true to who you are. It's very hard for the average person to stay true to themselves when they are constantly bombarded with images in the media of people doing amazing things, having amazing careers, and leading amazing lives. The images portrayed in the mass-media create these fairytale like fantasies of individuals who seem to dance through life with little or no effort at all. In turn, the illusion is created that it's something that anyone can do if they only put their mind to it.

This has the potential to create problems for people who truly desire to one day achieve an amazing lifestyle. The first problem is what's cut out of the equation: insane focus, intense dedication, and the sickening amount of work that went into creating the success behind the lifestyle being touted on the cover of the magazine. Cutting out the work element creates the illusion that, if that person can do it, then surely I can do it too. Meanwhile the average observer has no conception of what kind of sacrifice it took to get there. It's just one part of what makes up our instant gratification society: we believe that everything should just come to us. The disconnect is revealed when the person who is fantasizing about being Beyoncé discovers there is actual work involved. Not actual work, but a borderline obsessive dedication to the craft that requires a 12-hour day, every single day, for a decade, work ethic before you land a single gig. Mass-media leaves this part out because it's much less glamorous. Since the average person has become entrained to believe that everything should be handed to them, then it's not good marketing to reveal the gritty underside to success called *hard work*. It's much more profitable to continue to sell the fantasy of *that could easily be me*.

This is part of the reason why it's so important to be yourself because there are already 10,000 other people who are trying to be Beyoncé. Worse, what if you did put in the time and effort to learn how to sing like Beyoncé and actually became good at it? Now you are really good at singing like Beyoncé, but there is a problem: Beyoncé already exists! The world doesn't need, nor does it want another one of her. They are quite happy with having her. What the world does need is originality.

Now, if on the other hand, you saw her in concert, it lit a fire in your Soul, and you realized in your heart that you wanted to become a singer, that's completely different. If someone sparks a fire in your heart that lights the flame of desire then it's a valid calling. Where people go wrong is when they try to closely model themselves after a famous person doing something they think they want to do also.

It's especially evident in the world of self-help. There are now millions of people trying to become self-help experts who read one or two books and think, "That looks easy enough, I can do it too." The problem is they have no real life experience and are only doing it because they think they can. They aren't actually doing it because they are passionate about it. In a way, it's a sort of mental laziness. People who try to piggyback off of other people's dreams usually only clog up the arteries of the world with needless drivel. It's also why there will always only be the top 0.1% of productive people on the planet. This is because, long after all of the people who tried to copy other successful people failed, the dedicated ones who are authentically being themselves will carry on being themselves to the bitter end.

It's also a great way to see who is being authentic to themselves and who is not. The people who are being authentic to themselves will still be doing it while everyone else has moved on to the next trend.

RULES OF YOU

#1 Do Not Compare Yourself to Other People

Being authentic by staying true to who you are is one of the hardest things that you will ever do. There are so many pitfalls along the road to authenticity that it takes real, cultivated willpower to stay the course. One of the things that you will be tempted to do is to compare yourself to other people who are doing what you are doing. There are a lot of CEOs and companies who are constantly analyzing their competition and using it to try to improve their own products. And yet, true innovation has never come from comparison, not once, ever.

When you begin to compare yourself to other people who are doing what you want to do, it rarely ever enhances your own creativity or makes you better at what you do. If anything, what it does is to deemphasize your own innate talents and abilities. This is because when you observe other people you are seeing them utilize their own talents, strengths, and innate abilities. This does not help you to nurture yours, but instead sends you down a path where you begin to try to emulate who is already successful or what you believe is working. Now, instead of creating something new, you are trying to recreate something that someone else is doing. Since they are being themselves, and they are far better at being them than you will ever be, you are now fighting a losing battle.

For instance, if I wanted to be a professional speaker, the worst thing I could do would be to try to model myself after Anthony Robbins. For one, I am not a jump up and down, handclapping type of person. So right off the bat I am trying to emulate someone who I am not even really like. Second, I'm more of a calm, even-toned, speaker when it comes to getting on a stage and talking about something. If I continue trying to emulate Tony then now not only am I trying to compete with someone who is the best in the world at energizing people, but I'm also not honoring my own talents and gifts. I'm trying to be Tony instead of trying to be Chris. There is no way in hell that I can out "Tony" Tony.

Of course I could still be a motivational speaker if I wanted to. But there are a million different ways to motivate people without trying to be Tony. If I really wanted to emulate someone I would be better off trying to emulate Wayne Dyer. Even then, I'm never going to out "Wayne" Wayne. There will always only have ever been one Wayne Dyer. Yet, I could conceivably model myself after him to a point and still remain true to who I am. I could look at how he does what he does as a potential vehicle to deliver my own message. I wouldn't copy his message or try to teach what he teaches. Instead, I use his career as validation that I don't have to be the energizer bunny in order to motivate and inspire people. I can be me. I could even take it a step further by learning a bigger lesson from Wayne. He stubbornly refused to ever allow anyone to influence him to be anything other than exactly who he wanted to be.

Ralph Waldo Emerson said, "To be yourself in a world that is constantly trying to make you something else is the greatest accomplishment."

It's not the world's responsibility to allow you to be you though. It's your job to stay true to who you are and only use other people's accomplishments as inspiration to follow your own path. It's your job to never sellout to pop culture trends or to piggyback on other people's ideas. The world has enough copycats to last out the next 1,000 years of history. What it doesn't ever have enough of is authenticity. Originality.

So how do you know when you are really being yourself?

One way to know if you are really being yourself is if your idea or goal is exciting and stimulating. There is a massive difference between merely trying something out vs. being completely electrified and obsessed by the idea of it. You can always make something work halfway. But if you are reading this book then you are not merely trying to make something work a little bit. If you are reading this book then you are gearing up to become a global leader. You want your name to go down in the history books. So trying something is not what we do here.

What you want to connect with is what gets you excited and motivated. The question to ask yourself is: what is something that I know I would enjoy working on day and night, obsessively, trying to get exactly right? When you discover the craft that you know working on for the rest of your life will give you ultimate fulfillment then you are on track. The trick is to not get yourself caught up in overthinking it though. You don't want to be one of those people who, twenty years later, is still trying to find themselves. Sometimes what you have to do is just pick a direction and go with it. You can always correct the course along the way. There is nothing wrong with using someone else's success as a roadmap. The only danger is when you begin to follow it too closely or are doing it because you want to be like them. Then you have fallen out of authenticity and your potential success will slip away.

This is also one of the reasons why we have a tendency to

worship these amazing beings in the media. We are enthralled by how authentic they are. They capture our hearts and minds because they are themselves. We sense their purity and we crave it. We all secretly desire the simplicity and purity of mastering one craft or talent and making a good living at it.

The answer is that none of the super achievers of the world ever got there by trying to be someone they're not. None of the world's most innovative companies ever got to the pinnacle of success by trying to replicate an already existing business. If you want to join the ranks of the most productive people on the planet then you need to figure out definitively who you are, what is your business, what is your calling, and follow it to the very ends of the earth without worrying about if someone else is doing it differently or better than you.

Take Elon Musk who says, "I don't create companies for the sake of creating companies, but to get things done."

What he means is that he is never trying to compete with anyone, ever. Nor is he obsessed with trying to make money. What he is trying to do is fulfill a global need. He looks at the world, looks into the future, and sees what the world will be in need of. He then builds a company to try to answer that future need. He could care less about what anyone else is doing. That is not his focus. His focus is on answering global needs. Of course, this is how all great visionaries and entrepreneurs think. They don't look at businesses that are already in play and think, "I should do that too." What they do is to look at the world and see what is needed and try to innovate a way to fulfill that need. That is how the most productive people on the planet think in terms of business.

#2 Do Not Judge Yourself by Your Competition

Why is it so insanely difficult not to look at what the other gal is doing? Again, it's how we are programmed by mainstream mass-mind media. We're programmed to judge ourselves by how well our neighbor is doing. We're programmed to constantly look left and right for the validation that we're doing okay. This is how most of the big corporations have maintained their grip on supremacy for so long. They cater to the average person's need to judge their own progress in life by how the person next to them is doing. This means that you see your point of power as something external that exists outside of yourself. In this state it's much easier to manipulate you into mindless consumption.

Early on, when I was about five years into my professional writing career, once in a while I would see a new author emerge into the spotlight out of nowhere. It was not a case of being unaware of the many years of work this person had already put into writing beforehand. Rather, it was a case of someone having the exact right idea at the exact right time and deciding to put it down on paper (keyboard). In fact, I saw three of these writers come out of nowhere who, in reality, weren't even actual writers. They were simply people who were inspired by an idea and thought to make a nonfiction book about it. All three of them hit the NY Times bestseller lists. In the meantime, I continued to struggle to get people to buy my books. It was maddening to me and, if we're being completely honest here, I almost quit. Yes, I almost quit writing.

Why did I almost quit?

I almost quit because I fell into the biggest trap a creative person can fall into: I began to compare myself and my progress to other people. I fell into the trap of externalizing my power. When you begin to compare yourself to other people you are setting yourself up for a roller coaster ride of emotional highs and lows. One day you'll notice someone who has been at it for longer than you have, but who is not doing as well as you. That day you may feel validated because you know you're doing better than someone who is doing the same thing that you are. The next day, however, you may see someone who started three months ago and has already made their first one million sales. Now you'll feel like shit and want to quit.

The reality is that the greatest innovations, businesses, and art usually take a long time to come to fruition. They often take years of dedication, focus, and discipline before they become successful. The people who make history are the people who continue to show up and do the work, every single day, no matter what their competition is up to. In fact, they are often oblivious of what their competition is doing because they are so obsessed with perfecting their craft. This is the path of the most productive people on the planet.

In business it seems valid to observe the market place and watch your competition. Of course, if you have competition then you haven't been very innovative. If you are one among many other businesses then the fact is that you are probably not setting yourself up to occupy a page in the history books, unless you were the first one to start that kind of business and everyone else is simply trying to occupy the same market that you created. Then, you may be in line if you are solely dedicated to mastering your craft and not watching what everyone else is doing.

Some people rant and rave about watching the marketplace, observing trends, and continually checking up on their competition. This is the lesser path that relegates you to a kind of a rat race where you constantly have to respond to the potential disruptions in the marketplace caused by your competition. You are not a trendsetter, but a trend-responder. This is an inferior state of mind to get caught up in because anytime you have to respond to the market you are already a step behind.

So how do you get a step ahead?

The way that all of the greatest minds have gotten ahead and stayed ahead is by being innovative. Another name for the word innovative is *authentic*. Another word for authentic is *original*. And another word for original is *first*. You get ahead by being the first person in line. You get to be the first person in line by creating the damn line. Be the person who creates the line, not the one who sees everyone else in line and runs to get her place in it.

If you are an entrepreneur who enjoys building businesses as your passion, that's fine. But really, if you are just building businesses to build businesses, then you're already a step behind the curve. *Why?* You are not being innovative. You need a purpose, a driving force behind this need to build businesses. Your driving force should always, always, always be to create value. More specifically, your driving force should be to answer a specific need that will improve the quality of life on earth. If it doesn't then you need to recalibrate your neural network and figure out why you're doing what you're doing. The end goal should always be to create value by answering a need. Otherwise, you'll just never make it.

So what if you're an actor and you want to be famous? Wrong answer. The best actors in the world and, especially the elite 0.1%, are so insanely obsessed with perfecting their craft that you couldn't even conceive of it. If you want to be famous then you have fallen into the trap of comparing yourself to others and the need to stand out. You need validation. This is not how you gain mastery, but is rather how you fall into the gristmill of would-be actors.

When you are truly ready to master your craft then you need to be ready put all of your time, energy, and focus into what you're doing. As soon as you turn around to see what the other guy is doing you've lost the race. Instead, focus on being the absolute best version of you that you can possibly be. After all, people don't buy into businesses, they buy into character. Character is defined by focus, discipline, and innovation. You build zero character from paying attention to what the person next to you is doing. The only thing you build is a need to validate yourself, which detracts from your ability to develop willpower. If you continue to do this for long enough you will be reduced to a leaf blowing in the wind. What's worse is that it will be the wind created by people who are actual trendsetters and innovators. These are the ones who did not care about what anybody else was doing.

If you want to become one of the most productive people on the planet then you'll have to leave behind the need to look left or right. Keep your focus on what you're doing and keep doing the work and you'll get there.

#3 Stay True to Your Own Creative Flow

An incredibly important element of rising to the top 0.1% of the most productive people on the planet is the ability to establish and maintain your own creative flow. Your creative flow is the stream of creative energy that channels through you from your own higher intelligence. This is something that doesn't come naturally for most people and has to be nurtured and cultivated. As previously stated, you may even need to create the exact right work environment in order to stimulate your creativity. It's incredibly important to establish because the creative flow is your life's blood to innovation, as well as a profit.

It probably seems counterintuitive to you that the people who are making the biggest profits in the world are usually the most creative people on the planet. Creativity is an essential element to productivity. As an example, people almost always mistake productivity with over-mentalization when it comes to the creation of products to sell in the marketplace. Being productive does not mean to saturate the market with crappy toys or baubles that will ultimately fill the recycle centers of the world with an overabundance of used plastic. Being productive means the ability to tap into your creativity and provide solutions that are needed in the world. It means that you can turn on your creative engines and come up with efficient answers that will actually address real world needs.

Creating items that you are hoping to sell just to sell is not being productive. If anything, you are trying to think your way into someone's wallet. You may make a dollar or two doing this, but you are not making any sort of meaningful contribution to the world. Additionally, any profit you make will likely be short lived. You'll never make the history books or be known as an innovator. You will also never receive the feeling of having made a truly meaningful contribution to humanity, which is the greatest reward of engaging with this path.

If you want to be truly productive then you will need to be truly creative. The only thing more important than establishing your creative flow is to protect your creative flow. The reason this is so crucial is because, once you establish your creative flow, it's as if you have tapped into your own vein of gold in the virtual mountains of thought. The way to stake your claim is to keep your focus on what motivates and inspires you. The absolute second you look outside of your own creative flow you will have compromised it and, as a result, will take you valuable time and energy to reestablish it. Since your creative flow exists as a nonphysical entity there is no roadmap available to find it again. It can be elusive and take considerable time to establish in the first place. This is why only a fool will take their creative flow for granted by paying attention to current trends or what is selling in the market right now.

Every time you look at how someone else is doing something you dishonor your own creative flow. You have, once again, externalized your power source to something outside of you. The only time this is okay is if you are seeking motivation and inspiration. Otherwise, you are likely in the process of not trusting your own creative flow and supplanting it with someone else's instead. Ultimately, the more you do this, the less powerful you will become. The people who constantly try to mirror what is already established in art or the marketplace are some of the most powerless people on the planet.

There are always exceptions to every rule. For instance, if you are a mechanical engineer who loves to tinker with things. You love it so much that you buy things just to take them apart and see how they work. As a result, you stumble onto an innovative idea to improve on an already existing product. You come up with an idea to make the vacuum cleaner more powerful while simultaneously using less energy. The reason this is valid is because you are still following your passion: tinkering with mechanical stuff. What you are *not* doing is to attempt to reinvent the vacuum cleaner. What you *are* doing is feeding your own creativity, which is synonymous with doing what you love. Through your creative flow you have inadvertently created a valuable product for the marketplace.

However, this is different from what most people do. Most people see someone doing something and immediately forget about their own passion and creativity. They supplant their own inner creative flow with someone else's and then wonder why it never gains any momentum in the marketplace. This is for two reasons. First, it is not inspired by true creativity, which is the root of all innovation. Second, most of the people who do this are not interested in doing the work to perfect their craft, but are simply hoping they can copy success and become successful. This is not the path of the history maker but the path of the faint of heart and weak of mind.

If you are still here, reading away, then your path is different than everyone else's around you. Your path is to be considered as one of the creative geniuses of your time. Your path is to make history. History is never made by followers.

Create your own line and you'll always be the first one in it.

Lesson 8: Integration

1. Never compare yourself to anyone. This is one of the biggest mistakes you can make if you want to achieve uncommon success. The temptation is to compare and contrast yourself to people who have achieved the success that you dream of. It's one thing to attempt to adopt characteristics from successful people, but it's quite another to attempt to mimic their success. This only assures that you will never make it. *Why?* They've already done it. Instead, you need to remain true to who you are and bring your own highest vision of you to the world.

2. Never pay any attention to what your competition is up to. The reason is because this is not how world caliber innovations are brought to the planet. World caliber innovations are brought to the planet when an individual stubbornly sticks to their own ideas and never deviates, no matter what everyone else is doing. As soon as you look over at your competition and pay attention to what they're up to, you've lost. This is because you have externalized your power source. Now you've given your power over to your competition and have allowed what someone else is doing to influence your direction. Instead, realize that the

power is within you and waiting for you to tap into it. It always has been.

3. On your journey you are going to encounter all kinds of people doing all kinds of things. You'll see people doing things in the media and hear about it on the radio. You'll see people achieving amazing things who are in your field. No matter what though, you need to stay true to your own creative flow. No matter who is making what work in whatever way, you need to continue to do it in your way. Continue to allow your own feeling power to guide you and create what you want to create. Again, this is how true creativity and innovation is brought to the world: when an individual stubbornly ignores what everyone else is doing and continues to listen to their own inner voice.

Lesson 9

IT WILL HAPPEN WHEN IT'S READY TO HAPPEN

"No matter how prepared you think you are for it to happen, it never happens on your time. It always happens when it's supposed to happen."

—Curtis Brown

All of the lessons mentioned in this book thus far are behaviors that separate the top 0.1% from the rest of humanity. Each of them is powerful in its own way and assures that, upon implementation of this behavior, you will be walking a very different path than anyone else around you. Almost all of these lessons could be considered difficult to master and I am tempted to label each one as *the most difficult to master*. Yet, there really is one habit among them that is perhaps the most difficult to implement and follow through with. The ultimate separator of the highest level of productive people on the planet from everyone else is the ability to focus on doing the work and not on getting the results of the work. This means they are able to let go of attachment to outcome and simply continue to refine their craft.

It's easily one of the most difficult things for the average person to do, and it very quickly separates the individual who is truly ready to do the work from all the rest. It is the resolve that it won't happen when you want it to happen, but will only happen when it's ready to happen.

It seems simple enough and you could be tempted to overlook it: "Oh yeah sure, I know, I know, focus on the work, not the results," etc., etc. Yet I assure you that, at one point along your journey, you will begin to doubt and question what you are doing when you don't seem to be getting the results that you think you should. There will be at least one point, if not several, where you will make the mistake of thinking that the world does not want what you are offering because no one has showed up yet. This is a critical juncture because it's where the other 99.9% usually fall off of the radar and head back to their 9-5 jobs. This is what separates, definitively, the world class caliber super achievers from the rest of the world. They continue to show up every single day, even if they are the only one.

RULES OF WHEN

#1 It Doesn't Happen When You Want it to happen

This lesson is probably the most epic lesson for artists because artists really need people to show up and pay money to support their work. Every vocation needs people to show up and pay money for it in order to continue to exist and be successful. However, if no one is buying your books, showing up at your performances, purchasing your paintings, or going to your movies, then you're screwed. For artists who really want to achieve uncommon success it's the all or nothing road. This is because the successful artist needs to dedicate every second of the day to perfecting their craft. They need to become consumed by it. It also means that for most artists who walk this path there will be some lean years ahead.

It can easily be the same for the aspiring CEO of a new startup or an entrepreneur working on a new product or invention. Most I've seen aren't starving like many of the artists I know, however there can easily be some lean years in store for them as well.

Or, perhaps you are an aspiring fighter who is training MMA. If you want to make it into the UFC then you will have to train your ass off every single day, for hours at a time. This means that you might have to live in a basement or in your car, literally.

If you are walking down any of these paths then it means you will be tested, down to your very core.

How strong are you? Can you weather the storm? Can you make the herculean amounts of sacrifice that you will inevitably be asked to make? Will you be able to watch as other people around you enjoy getting new clothes, new cars, take trips, go on vacations, and have enough money to buy Christmas presents for everyone they love while you continue to toil on with the creation of your dreams? There comes a moment in time when you will be forced to dig deep, deeper than you ever have before. You will question everything, even your very existence. You will wonder why you are here and what is the point of it all? You will feel like giving up and, for many, this is the breaking point. Yet, from the ashes one will always rise and, if you're still reading, then it's likely to be you.

It's not the one who can get knocked down and get back up that makes it through this time period. No my friend, not even. It's the one who can get knocked down 1,000 times and still get back up. *You want uncommon success?* Then you are in for a battle. This battle is not fought anywhere external though, but is an ongoing war that is fought within. This is the war for the freedom of expression of your Soul and will last a lifetime. The rewards for those who are eventually able to win this war are of the magnitude and degree that most of us only dream of. It's just that most people could never possibly conceive of what goes into the making of the most productive people on the planet.

In order to even begin to conceive of this type of success you will need to accept that your only job is to show up and do the work. If you are inventing a product then you will create the blueprint. Then you will refine the blueprint. Then you will refine the blueprint some more. Then you will develop the prototype. It will not work. You will build another one. It will not work. You will build yet another one. It will not work. Then you will redesign the blueprint. Then you will redesign the blueprint again. Then you will rebuild the prototype. It will not work. Then you will rebuild the prototype again. Then... do you see where this is going? This is part of the process of making history. In order to make history you need to have an uncommon and borderline insane dedication to achieving mastery of your craft. Whether you are a politician, a business owner, an inventor, an actor, a singer, a fighter, a CEO, or a poet, you need to be ready to weather the storm. You need to be willing to fail at least 1,000 times knowing that you might get it right on the 1,001 try.

Think about all of the things that we would be robbed of in our modern world if the greatest innovators in history had all believed that it was supposed to happen on their own time table? I'm assuring you that we would have virtually none of the greatest innovations and inventions that we currently take for granted. Not one of them. We would not have asphalt roads, water faucets, flushing toilets, ovens, gas burners, lighting in our homes, central air, LCD screens, computers, coffee grinders, movie theaters, airplanes, and comfortable seats at Starbucks. In the modern world we take advantage of dozens, perhaps even hundreds of amazing innovations every day and barely take notice. We take for granted the amazing, obsessed, and insane individuals it took to create our everyday walkabout world. Each and every one of these neurotically obsessed geniuses had to give up on the idea that it was going to happen when they wanted it to happen. They all had to accept that it would only happen when it was ready to happen.

Letting go of the time table of when you think it's supposed to happen frees you up to create the absolute best version of your product that you possibly can. Only then are you also able to subsequently begin to rise up to the level of uncommon success that is denoted by the numeric value of 0.1%.

You don't get to decide when it happens, no matter what you've been told about creating timelines on your goal achievements. Timelines are for people who have not committed to doing the work, every day, forever. Timelines are for people who need to create a sense of urgency in order to show up and do the work. The timeline of the super achiever is a much greater one that is being orchestrated by something much greater than you. Accept this and move on.

#2 Don't get caught up in the numbers

This is as equally difficult to do. When you first launch your app you will be tempted to check downloads, not every day, but every second. It's difficult to not want to continue to check the numbers every 30 seconds to see how many people are downloading it. The problem is that doing this never helps you in any productive way. If anything, it will only create an emotional rollercoaster that spikes when you finally see a download and then takes a huge dip when you realize it's the only one of the day. Obsessing over the number of downloads or sales you are making is the quickest ride straight into a prescription for Xanax. It will make you anxious, depressed, and eventually manic. It's very difficult to sustain any level of productivity if you are creating continual emotional highs and lows for yourself. In fact, it's virtually impossible.

The world's most productive people know this and will vehemently avoid looking at the numbers at all costs. They are more concerned with the perfection of the craft than they are with the initial sales of the product. While other people are fretting over what they perceive to be a bad launch, the super achievers are still hard at work refining their product and making adjustments. They know that when they get it just right, the world will come knocking. They also know that the numbers are not a true reflection of the value of their creation. There are simply way too many factors at play to make that kind of assumption or determination so early in the game.

So while the average person has already given up because their creation was not an instant success, the world's most productive are still in the workroom blasting away at the perfection of their work of art. In fact, they could care less about the numbers since their focus isn't on numbers at all, but to make the world a better place. They are aware of the fact that when they get it just right it will change the face of the planet. This is when you truly cease to worry about the numbers because you cannot count the hordes of people standing outside your doors waiting to get in.

This is the gap between the one who tries to work in vain on the numbers vs. the super productive individual who continues to refine the product. One will eventually make some sales while the other will eventually make history.

Which pathway sounds more appealing to you?

One of the reasons why there are so few super achievers is because of all the hard choices you have to make to become one. One of them is the choice not to focus upon the numbers. You may think I am, yet again, insane to perpetuate this philosophy. I assure you though that if you research any of the greatest innovations of the past 100 years, you will discover the same underlying insanity is responsible, every single time. Part of that insanity is the sole focus on the perfection of a world changing invention, work of art, or piece of music.

You simply cannot have it both ways. You cannot create something that will change the world while you are stressed out about the numbers. Even in the cases exemplified by an individual who was also good at selling their invention or product, they were really only spreading the message.

It's what happens when you have something that you have put your heart and soul into: you wind up engaged less in selling and more in sharing. Because you know, in your heart, that you put everything you had into it, your confidence and energy will shine through when you speak about it. This is part of the magic of why Steve Jobs was able to sell Macs and iPhones so well. He knew that he had amazing products so he didn't really need to sell anything. He only needed to share the message. This is an important distinction between focusing on the numbers vs. sharing your invention. Of course, you never really know what's going to happen. You only know in your heart what your mission is.

Do I want to make the world a better place or do I want to make sales?

If you are focused on making sales, then you are focused on the short game. If you are focused on changing the world, then not only are you focused on the long game, but you are focused on the same intention as the top 0.1% of world caliber achievers. None of them were ever focused on the short game. In fact, the short game never existed to them. Every single one of them was focused on creating something of permanent and lasting value that would change the way we perceive the world.

When you make this your goal you are elevating yourself to the level of the most productive people on the planet. Until this is your goal you are aiming too low to make the cut.

By this point in the book we've no doubt thinned the herd considerably. This is because the majority of the population is addicted to the "shiny object" syndrome. It means that the average person responds to life much in the same way as a gold fish does; whatever the shiniest thing is outside of the bowl gets your attention. In fact, a recent study found that the average person's attention span is less than that of a gold fish.

You heard that right.

If this is the case, then you know what I am about to say: very few people have the courage, dedication, discipline, and stamina to walk this path. If you are always looking for the shiny object then you do not have what it takes. This is because you have fallen prey to the need to be constantly entertained by someone or something. In turn, this means that your attention span is shorter. In turn, this means that you now have the need for instant gratification. If you have that need then when you begin to work on your project, you will also need to see some sales. When this doesn't happen you will instantly give up. That is, if you have a goldfish type personality.

However, if you are still reading then you may be who I'm looking for. You may be the one in a million, absolute badass, who can weather all storms to ultimately fulfill the Soul-level calling that has been tugging at your heart for an eternity.

So forget the numbers and do what you came here to do.

#3 Stay Nonattached to the Outcome

This lesson is very similar to, and an extension of, the first two on this topic. The reason why I am going to continue to pound this lesson into your brain is due to its critical nature concerning your ability to achieve your goals. Nonattachment to outcome is an absolutely essential element to joining the ranks of the most productive people on the planet. If you are a world changer, then the journey ahead of you will probably be long and arduous and will make you question yourself at every turn. You are in for days, weeks, months, and most likely even years of dedication before you see the payoff. What it means is that, not only do you need to develop your willpower and self-discipline, but you additionally need to develop the ability to stay nonattached to the outcome.

Most people associate the term nonattachment with giving up or not caring if you ever achieve your goals. Of course, nothing could be further from the truth. Nonattachment simply means that you are letting go of the when and the how it will eventually happen. You are letting the nonphysical aspects of your own higher intelligence work in tandem with Mother Nature to fulfill the manifestation of your goals. People who are nonattached usually exhibit more of a deeper knowing and faith that it will happen than those who are strongly attached to outcome.

Why?

It's because how strongly attached you are to an outcome indicates the more fear you have that it's not going to happen. The more you are pushing for something to happen the more likely it will be that you are doing so because you don't really believe that it will actually happen.

There is nothing wrong with pursuing a goal and being aggressive with putting it out into the world. However, if you are strongly attached to outcome then it probably means you will wind up depressed a good part of the time. This is because, at the level of the world changer, it takes a lot of failures before you find the success you are seeking. Thus, if you are strongly attached to an outcome, then you will take each of these failures very hard. This puts you right back on the emotional rollercoaster and compromises your ability to stay productive. Now you are moving up and down and up and down the emotional ladder. In turn, this will move you from a productive state to a dysfunctional state and back and forth between the two. What's worse is that it will use up your valuable time and energy while you attempt to emotionally recover and reclaim your productive state of mind. Every time this occurs it puts you behind the game.

If you want to stay productive then you simply cannot allow this to happen. The most productive people on the planet never take it personally and part of the reason why is because they are nonattached to the outcome. They remain focused on the work, knowing that it will happen when it's ready to happen, and not one second before. They show up, do the work, go home, let it go, and go to sleep. Then they get up the next day and do it all over again.

This is also why many great spiritual teachers have said over and over, "Do what you love." But, I have another way of looking at it. Since that phrase has confused millions of people by sending them on the wild goose chase to try to find themselves, I say, "Quit looking." Instead, pick a direction and never look back. Just make sure that you enjoy doing it enough to want to be the very best in the world at it. You will always question your path no matter what. That's just part of the equation. It's a matter of whether you allow yourself to be swayed by the inner doubts and thoughts that will attempt to sidetrack you.

This is also where nonattachment comes into play quite nicely. If you are nonattached then you will be less likely to allow these inner demons to hold any power over you. This is because when you are nonattached you don't pay any attention to the need for externally validating factors. Money, sales, applause, approval from friends, none of it matters to the dedicated innovator or artist. Your nonattachment frees you up to more fully focus on being the absolute best that you can possibly be. It's ironic that the less attached you are to outcome, the more likely you will wind up being one of the best the world has ever seen.

Nonattachment also helps you tap into the nonlinear domain of thought. This is because when you are attached to outcome you believe that you are the one responsible. Specifically, the "you" who is responsible is your linear mind. The more attached you are to the outcome the more likely that you will begin to utilize your linear thinking mind to the exclusion of your nonlinear mind. This means that you are cutting yourself off from the origin of all innovation and creativity. You cannot possibly mentally think a world caliber innovation into being. You must be inspired to create something that changes the face of the world. In turn, this can only come from the nonlinear domain. This can only happen when you are nonattached to outcome.

The paradox is apparent: obsessively dedicated to the point of being labeled as "insane" by the people who know you vs. being apparently indifferent to the fact of when and how it eventually happens. *Do you care if it ever happens?* Of course you do. Even the most nonattached person wants it to happen. Yet, the irony is that the more nonattached you are then the more likely it is to happen. Again, this is because through nonattachment, you are more likely to enter into the nonlinear domain of thought and access the endless treasure trove of creativity and innovation that awaits you.

Some people refer to this state as "patiently impatient." It means that you want it to happen, but you are willing to allow it to happen when it's ready to happen. Some people will be able to read this and understand what it means and begin to loosen their mental grip on the outcome. Other people may intellectually understand this, but will still not be able to actualize the state of nonattachment. This is why we have the technique of meditation and a big part of the reason why it was created in the first place.

Through meditation, not only will you be able to enter into the nonlinear domain of thought, but you will also be able to actualize the state of nonattachment to outcome. This is great news because the more nonattached you are then the more focused you can remain on your objective, which is to change the world.

Many of the top 0.1% are actual meditation practitioners: Steve Jobs, David Lynch, Russell Simmons, Oprah Winfrey, Ray Dalio, Rupert Murdoch, Arianna Huffington, Jeff Bridges, Marc Benioff, Joachim Chissano, Katy Perry, Rick Goings, Sheryl Crow, Ellen Degeneres, Cameron Diaz, Yukio Hatoyama, Andrew Cherng, Jerry Seinfeld, Martin Scorsese, Barry Zito, and George Lucas.

Do you get the picture?

If you look through the list you see actors, producers, CEOs, presidents, comedians, and world famous entrepreneurs. This is no ordinary list; this is a list some of the people who have achieved the top 0.1% of their game. There are hundreds more I could add onto this list as well. But this, by itself, should sufficiently convince you as to the efficacy of the power of meditation. Since one of the primary benefits of meditation is nonattachment to outcome then you can begin to connect the dots on your own. It means that nonattachment to outcome will help you to soar to heights undreamed of. It will help you to allow bigger results than you may have previously been able to conceive of make their way into your life. It will also allow you to focus on the only thing that matters, which is doing the work.

Creating a state of nonattachment will help you to allow the wellspring of the nonlinear domain to enter into your life and eventually enable you to join the ranks of the most productive people on the planet. It will also keep the Xanax at bay.

Lesson 9: Integration

1. This is a crazy one, but you need to give up trying to force it happen. This does not mean that you aren't working hard every day, but it does mean that you need to quit hoping that today will be the day. The reason is that it never happens exactly when you want it to happen. It only happens when it's ready to happen. The good news is this frees you up to do the work.

2. There will come a time when you will be tempted to begin to check the numbers. You'll be checking for sales, downloads, looks, views, opt-ins, purchases, etc. But, if you get caught up in the numbers, then it will do two things. First, it will make you become neurotic, which takes you out of a productive state. Second, it could easily give you a false positive or a false negative. It's also possible that your first product is only the preparation for the next one, which is the one that will hit. You just can't know. So don't get caught up in the numbers.

3. It's not attachment to outcome that's your enemy. We all have attachment to outcome. Rather, it's extreme attachment to outcome that's the problem. This means that when it doesn't take off right away you will get depressed. It also

means that you put yourself on an emotional rollercoaster: experiencing highs when things seem to be going well and lows when they are not. The most productive people on the planet are too focused on doing the work to be worried about results. When you continue to show up, do the work, and remain nonattached to outcome is when you are on track to one day be hailed as a genius.

Lesson 10

NEVER GIVE UP

"It always seems impossible until it's done."
—Nelson Mandela

This is probably the most touted lesson when it comes to studying, researching, and ultimately preaching lessons about how the world's most productive achieved their status. The average person will parrot out this lesson as if they have any idea of the true meaning: *never give up!* It's a powerful lesson and we're all well aware of it by now. But, to be honest, very few people really understand this lesson. It's another item in a long list which fall under the heading: *easy to say, hard to do.* Or perhaps this list: *do as I say, not as I do.*

Right?

Yes, we've all heard someone tell us not to give up who, themselves, have given up on every single project they've ever tried to execute. Despite appearances, it's never been my objective to be a cynic in this book. Rather, it IS my objective to mentally train you how to achieve a level of success that no one in your immediate circle could ever possibly conceive of. Since they couldn't conceive of it then, when they say something like never give up, it has very little meaning. What this does is to slowly but surely subconsciously erode the original intention of that phrase. Worse, if you had a parent who said this to you while simultaneously never exerting any effort to achieve anything meaningful, then it could have a detrimental effect on your subconscious.

This is, unfortunately, why it doesn't pay to listen to 99.9% of people who you run into on the street or who you know personally in your life. This is true at least if you ever plan on achieving a level of success that will put your name in the headlines.

So what does it really mean to never give up?

To never give up means that after you have fallen down so many times you are bloody, you don't have a single dime to your name, and you are all alone because everyone else has gotten tired of your antics, that you can get back up and carry on without a nanoseconds delay. In fact, not only do you get back up, but you do so with a smile on your face and a whistle on your lips. The Titanic may have just sunk, Krakatoa may have just erupted, the stock market may have just crashed, and your house may have just burnt to the ground. Not only does this not stop you, but it doesn't even phase you. Your mood is still dapper and you are still on track.

Another way to say "never give up" is "to be unstoppable."

The most productive people on the planet never entertain the idea that anything could ever possibly deny them from achieving their dreams. There is no option where they give up and get a 9-5 job. There is no option where they fall back on plan B. There is no option where they run out of money and have to quit.

The phrase "if there is a way, they will find it" doesn't even come close to this mentality. Rather, it's more like "there is never not a way." Since these insanely obsessed world caliber achievers never give themselves any other option then they will eventually always achieve what they set out to do: make the world a better place. When you have a singular point of vision and it's all you ever see then it will eventually become a reality for you. Inherently, all of the world class caliber achievers know this and will only ever allow themselves to see the one outcome: *success.*

Thus to never give up is a bit of an oxymoron for the world's most productive. It implies duality, which means there is an actual option to give up. Since this does not exist for the world's most productive then it's irrelevant. But, it's irrelevant for them, not for you. You have not yet adopted this mentality or you would not be reading this book. Adopted isn't truly accurate in this sense either. This mentality is more like an iron-forged burn mark on your Soul. What you are looking for here is to accept that there is no Plan B. Plan B merely distracts from Plan A. In other words, your eye needs to stay on the ball every second of the game and the game is your life's work.

Am I getting a little heavy here?

I am may be starting to sound a little ominous. The truth of the matter is that I know what it takes and there is no middle ground. So if I have to alienate a couple folks in order to motivate the ones who will weather the storm, then I accept it. It's not my goal to alienate you, but it is my goal to make sure you really understand what this book is about and why you are reading it. If you are reading it to try to knock out a couple goals and become a little more efficient then you're reading it for the wrong reasons. This isn't a "take what you want and leave the rest" type of book.

This is a do or die, kill or be killed type of book. My desire is to ignite your inner Soul flame, stoke it a little bit, and then turn it into a raging inferno that will carry you straight into a level of achievement that carves your name into the pages of immortality. Hopefully that wasn't too heavy for you.

RULES OF NEVER GIVE UP

#1 A Failure is an Opportunity to Learn

Part of the reason why the most productive people on the planet never quit is because they have developed a unique ability. This is the ability to turn every failure into an opportunity to learn something. They rarely, if ever, become emotionally upset when something doesn't work. Instead, when they fail, they break it down, analyze it, turn it upside down, take it apart, and look at it from every angle.

What did I do wrong? What could I do differently? What did I miss?

These super beings take it upon themselves to figure out where they went wrong, learn from the mistake, and try again. In fact, this may very well be the simplified version of the formula as to how they achieve world class status. They merely allow themselves to make mistakes without judgment. They never criticize themselves or their team. They always take full responsibility for the failure, break it apart, and analyze it until they know what went wrong. There is no demise, disaster, or catastrophe. For them it's no big deal, but simply a part of the process.

The average person will take the failure much differently. They make it personal, as if they, themselves, are a failure. They allow themselves to feel unworthy, as if they are not smart enough, good enough, or deserving enough. They create a story around the failure that says "I'm not cut out for this." It seems small but amounts to a massive difference between the average person and the most productive people on the planet.

So this begs the question: what if you were able to not take things so personally? What if, when you failed at something, you never let it bother you? You may think this is not such a big deal, but it is one of the biggest separators between the average person and the world class person. It's the ability to not take it personally or create a self deprecating story around it. The world's most productive people carry on as if nothing out of the ordinary happened at all.

For them it is not a matter of *if*, it is a matter of *when*.

On your quest to achieve your dreams and live a life that most people will only dream of you need to begin to look at every failure as an opportunity to learn. Failures need to become your teachers, nothing more. You need to remove all other meaning from the word *failure* aside from *learning lesson*. Each failure is a stepping stone that brings you closer to the vision you are trying to create. Every failure learned from makes you into a better version of yourself. After 100 failures you should be a version of yourself that's 100 times better.

#2 Changing Your Approach is Okay

On the other hand, there is an option that's acceptable to execute if something isn't working. Sometimes you will run into a wall and it will seem insurmountable. You will be confounded because no matter what you do you remain frustrated as attempts to get around it continue to elude you.

Failure is not an option in this instance because it implies that you are quitting. Since your mission is to arrive one day at the top 0.1% of the world's most productive then quitting does not exist for you. However, there is another option: *change your approach*. It's okay and even valid to change your approach if nothing is working. If you have tried everything in your arsenal, meditated on it, let it go, brainstormed it with your team, and nothing is working, then it may be time to change your approach.

Changing your approach does not mean that you are giving up your goal, vision, or dream. It simply means that you are aware there is more than one way to achieve your vision and you're flexible enough to try new tactics.

Bruce Lee said, "Be like water."

What he meant is that the ability to be flexible and allow yourself to change is superior to the state of being rigid and unchanging. It also means that you can learn new things and evolve yourself. Any time you allow yourself to try a new approach you are also allowing yourself to evolve and become an enhanced version of yourself. Most of the greatest minds in history were known for their continual study and evolution of their craft. They continued to focus on the one thing, but they also evolved as their approach shifted in order to continue to be the best in the world at it.

Another way of saying this is that the world's most productive people are all able to adapt to their environment and their circumstances. When they encounter an incredibly difficult obstacle they will still eventually overcome it. However, one of the ways they will overcome it is to change their approach and learn a new strategy. The vision remains the same, but the pathway to get there may change.

Can you imagine a commercial airline pilot who is trying to land in Florida, but is blocked by a small storm front? So, instead of navigating a way around it, he simply turns around and heads all the way back to San Francisco? In his mind the storm represents an insurmountable obstacle so he simply gives up and heads home. This is the way that many people in the world operate. When something doesn't work they simply give up. What's worse is if they've heard the phrase "it wasn't meant to be" somewhere along the road of life. If they've heard this phrase then it may be all they need in order to throw in the towel and head home.

Conversely, the world's most productive never dream of entertaining the idea that it wasn't meant to be. That phrase or ideology doesn't exist for them and if you attempt to propagate it you will get kicked out of their circle permanently. There are many wishy-washy phrases and philosophies touted by the masses that will validate your inability to stay the course and reach your objective. But they are for the masses; they are not for you. So the phrases "meant to be" or "not meant to be" no longer apply to you, never again.

I used to think like that. I used to think "well it was just not meant to be." I used that phrase to get out of trying to accomplish big goals or anything that required hard work and sacrifice. I used to think that if it was "meant to be" that it would be easy. The fact is that nothing could be further from the truth. To be sure, the more it was meant to be, probably the harder the road will be ahead. This is, at least, if you consider the things in life that were meant to be are all things that have changed the way we view the world.

Can you imagine how different the world would look if the most productive people on the planet had allowed themselves to think like this?

One thing for sure is that we would not have electrical lighting in our homes or anywhere else for that matter.

Why?

Because Thomas Edison failed 10,000 times before creating the light bulb. 10,000 times! That is 10,000 times that he could have self-validated his need to quit with the phrase "it was not meant to be." So it's probably time to shit-can that phrase once and for all. Remember, the roadmap to uncommon success is dotted with tons of roadblocks and failures. It's your job to change your approach by building a bridge over the ravine, chiseling a tunnel through the mountain, or hacking out a new path through the jungle. If it was not meant to be then you would not have been put on the planet.

#3 The Last Leg of the Journey

Why is the last mile of the race the most profitable mile of the race?

It's because it's the least populated mile. There are the least number of actors, entrepreneurs, athletes, and innovators in the last mile. Most everyone else has fallen off long ago making the last mile seem like a ghost town. For the people who make it, they get the uncommon distinction of joining the most productive people on the planet and having their names put in the history books. They also get the lion's share of the profits because nobody else has the stamina to run the long race. With today's mass media culture basically entraining people to believe that everything should come to them at the touch of a button, in the very instant they need it, uncommon success will become even more uncommon.

Mentally, the barrier to entry will begin to get higher and higher. This is not because it takes any more effort than it used to in order to reach heights undreamed of. It will always take a herculean amount of effort. No, the reason is because the average person is becoming more and more robotized and thinks less and less independently for themselves. It's why the gap between the super achievers and the average person will appear to grow bigger and bigger. It's not the fault of the world caliber achievers. Rather, it has to do with the mental laziness of the average person to believe whatever is told to them and take whatever is given them.

So what is your job?

If you're still reading and have been able to deal with some of the heaviness that I've blasted you with, then your job is simply to carry on. Your job is to not quit right before you get to the last mile. Your job is to not be swayed by the news, video games, TV, pop culture, trends, friends, or family. Your job is to become the rock in the middle of the storm. Your job is to become so mentally and emotionally solid that you are immovable. Your job is to become unstoppable in the pursuit of bringing something amazing to the planet. Your job is to persevere to the very end.

Have I reached the right person?

If you are ready to engage with this journey at all costs and never give up no matter what then I probably have the right individual. If you consider yourself to be somewhat obsessive, slightly insane, and inordinately stubborn then I most likely have the right person. If you want your name to go down in the history books then I definitely have the right person. If you want the world to have been a better place because you were in it, then yes, you are the one I am looking for.

Virtually every single one of the world's most productive people have all of the above mentioned qualities. They all have this unusual set of characteristics that make them able to continue on when every other single person in the world would has quit long ago. It's this very ability that has some people posing another question: is there a special set of circumstances that go into the creation of making an individual who will never give up? In other words, were there unique environmental circumstances during the childhoods of the world changers we know today that made them who they are?

Here is my answer: *does it really matter?* What if there were special circumstances behind every single one of them? What if we found out that they were all born into the exact right set of environmental circumstances to make them who they are? What if none of them would have made it to superstardom had it not been for the abusive father, the continual shifting of foster homes, or the mother who was incredibly strict? What if being born into abject poverty was what it took to motivate you to desire to rise to uncommon heights of success?

Do you see how this creates a problem for you? The problem is that you could use this data to validate never achieving anything meaningful. Another way of framing it is to say that you can always find a reason to do or not do something. There will always be data available to back up whatever you believe is possible or impossible to do in this world. You will always be able to find someone to either agree or disagree with your beliefs in limitation. You will always be able to find an article in the paper to back you up if you don't want to do it. Conversely, you will always be able to find the story of someone who did it with much less than you.

The choice is yours: what do you want to believe in? *Limitlessness or limitation?* Both options are present and available for you to choose from and both can be validated. It's just that there are millions who believe in one and only a handful who believe in the other.

If you want to believe in limitlessness then you will have to drown out the noise of the masses, get ready to do the work, and then not quit before you hit the last mile.

If you follow the lessons in this book, 100% without fail, you will become 1 in 10,000,000, literally. Your life will change in ways that you could not possibly conceive of. You will gain access to experiences that you've never dreamed of having before. You will become uncommon. You will also be considered amongst the most productive people on the planet and gain your own page in the history books. Most importantly of all, you will have made the world a better place by adhering to a set of lessons that force you to give the very best you possibly can, no matter what.

These lessons will make you into the most powerful possible version of yourself that you could ever become. From here, you will be in a position to bring the highest possible contribution to the planet and humanity that you are possibly capable of.

This is your destiny and now is the time. Get to work.

Lesson 10: Integration

1. From this day forward you will look at the word failure in a completely new way. Every time you do something that doesn't work it will become an opportunity to learn. It's not that you won't fail, but that you won't ever quit. Now each failure brings you closer to joining the ranks of world caliber achievers. It becomes a learning lesson that enhances your skills and abilities.

2. One thing commonly misunderstood by the masses is the difference between quitting your dreams vs. changing your approach. The most productive people on the planet know the difference and utilize this difference constantly. There are endless ways to achieve your vision and you may have to try a couple different routes to get the destination.

3. The reason the last leg of the journey is the most successful is because 99.9% of people who set out on this journey never make it. This is why there are only 0.1% of the people at this level of success. What this tells you is that you need to keep going, especially when it gets rough. It's just past the storm that you find the secret island with all the treasure. Most turn back, but you will keep going and enjoy uncommon success.

Lesson 11

YOU ARE NEVER DONE CREATING

"Business opportunities are like buses, there's always another one coming."

—Richard Branson

The last item on the list of lessons that separate world caliber achievers from everyone else has to do with a permanent mental gear that you will need to shift into. This is the "never done creating" gear. It's why the super productive people are so super productive, because they are never trying to get done. This is a subtle, yet powerful lesson. It's because when you are trying to get it done then you are not really trying to perfect your craft. You are more focused on the rewards that potentially come with completing the project.

The world's most productive people are always trying to perfect their craft because they love the act of refining their craft. If you have two people side by side working on the same project, and one is trying to finish it while the other one is taking it apart again for the 100th time, which one do you think will provide the most value upon completion? Right, it's going to be the one that has been taken apart 100 times and rebuilt 100 times and refined another 100 times. It's not going to be the one that has been pushed through and is sitting on the sales room floor that is "acceptable." It's going to be the incredibly refined and perfected one that people have had to wait another 9 months for. It's going to be the one that has the extra 10,000 hours of work and dedication put into it.

So another name for this gear that you need to shift into could be: *love of the craft.*

Although part of doing the work is not very fun at all, because you have to work through the resistance of doing the work, perfecting and refining your craft should feel very fulfilling. In other words, when you are refining your craft it should feel as if you are doing what you want to be doing. It's a paradox because it does feel like work. Yet, there is an incredible difference between showing up at a 9-5 that you hate vs. sitting in your garage and working on a new type of electrical engine. They are both work, but only one is considered a *job.*

This is why another way of saying "doing the work" is to say "working through resistance." The rewards of working through resistance are that you get to do something meaningful and that you get to choose your own destiny. Waking up in the morning to go to a job you hate could involve resistance. But it's not true resistance. True resistance is what keeps us from living the life of our dreams. It's what keeps us living the same life over and over again, every day. The feeling of going to a job you hate is your Soul telling you that you are missing out on the opportunity to actualize yourself. The feeling that you have, which could be depression, anxiety, or frustration, is your resistance to your Soul's calling for yourself.

So they are both resistance, but one has to do with continuing to do the work, while the other one is avoiding having to take responsibility for your life path. If you are still feeling that kind of depression or anxiety because you have not pulled the trigger then it means that the fear is winning. By now in this book I am expecting this to be a nonissue for you. However, if it is still an issue, ask yourself this question: am I really happy to let my life go by knowing that I will be in this exact same situation ten years from now?

The answer should not be a "no." It should be a "hell fucking no!"

Right.

Once you move through the resistance of showing up every day to do the work, then the final gear shift is accepting that you never get it done. This is your new, permanent state of being, which is ultra productive. Congratulations, you made it.

RULES OF NEVER GETTING IT DONE

#1 Retirement is Never the Goal

L ooking forward to your retirement? Planning for that day when you never have to work again?

Think again my friend, because that all just got flushed down the toilet. You see, you picked up this book and started reading. Then you did something even more incredible: you kept reading to the brutal end. That takes some serious mental endurance because you've had to work through every single one of your subconscious sabotage mechanisms to make it this far. If you've read through to this point then it means you have a certain caliber that the rest of the population lacks. It means that you may very well be made of steel.

It also means that the idea of retirement, well, it went "bye-bye."

Why?

Because the world's most productive people never even dream of the thing. It's a dirty word in their book that never enters into any conversation, ever. Retirement is for the average mind to contemplate, hope for, or attempt to plan for. It is not for world caliber goal achievers though. It means that it's not for you.

Want to achieve uncommon success? Then you will need

to shit-can the term 'retirement' and exorcise it from your vocabulary as if it were some rare form of virus that will infect your life with a deadly disease. The disease in this case is mental laziness and fear. To hope to make it through life, usually putting in time at a job that you don't really enjoy, only to sit around and wait for death, involves a certain type of insanity. It's mass-mind insanity.

Your days of dreaming of retirement are over. Instead, you will move forward, from creation to creation, enhancing the quality of lives of millions of people on the planet with your gifts. Your only mission is to make this planet a better, happier, more efficient, healthier, creative, and more fun place to be. It isn't to vegetate in front of the TV until your physical body atrophies away into nothing.

So now you know, retirement is a dirty word, and no longer fits into any of your plans.

#2 You Continue to Develop New Ideas

Focusing on one thing for so long has now done something unexpected and amazing for you: it has opened a lot of new doors. It's incredible, strange, and even ironic; yet, it's still true. Somehow, focusing exclusively on only one thing has provided more opportunities than you could ever have conceived of.

Why?

It's because when you've focused on one thing for so long, you get really, really good at it. Then, the strangest thing happens: the world comes to your doorstep. Then, something even stranger happens: you get tons of new opportunities.

It's weird because you have put all of your eggs into one basket and, yet now, it almost appears as if you have opportunities coming from multiple baskets. It's some really strange reverse engineering that Mother Nature is using on you here. However, what's true is true, and this is true.

Opportunities will continue to arise and you will continue to use these opportunities to develop new ideas. This means that you will continue to develop new ideas that spin off of your one thing.

If you are a song writer, then you will continue to write new songs. If you are an entrepreneur, then you will continue to develop new business ideas. If you are an inventor, then you will continue to develop new inventions. If you are an athlete, then you will continue to train for the next competition.

People will come to you more frequently and want you to work on a project for or with them. So fine, do it. At this point you've earned the credibility as well as the immense paycheck that comes from people chasing after you to get you to work on their projects.

You are now in a continual state of expansion where your one idea leads to the next and the next. Your consciousness has expanded through your daily meditation and focus and you are now able to tap into the nonlinear domain of thought on a regular basis. Ideas flow to you and through you almost as if you have a direct line into the collective unconscious.

Allow it to continue to flow. This is your life force energy. Continue to harness it and let it build up. As one of the most productive people on the planet you now oscillate between the linear and nonlinear domains of thought on a daily basis. Some people refer to you as a genius, but you know better. You have simply followed a formula to arrive at a set destination which would be the same for anyone with the courage to do so. This means that you are not special. You are just insanely and obsessively dedicated to staying ultra creative. It also means that you have a permanent seat amongst the top 0.1% of achievers in the world.

#3 If You Do Master One Craft, Move on to the Next

Occasionally, some of the world's most productive people will come into absolute mastery of their craft. They have focused so exclusively on refining and perfecting the one thing that they may have run out of room to grow. They may feel as if they have maxed out their potential in one area and desire to expand their creativity and consciousness as well. When this happens you may see them jump from one area of creativity to another. It usually also means they have become ultra successful, which gives them some leeway to experiment.

If you have mastered your craft, achieved uncommon success, and joined the top 0.1% of the world's most productive people, then it's completely valid to desire to continue to challenge yourself. This is when you see a music producer like Curtis Brown start a clothing line. Or you see Richard Branson start the Council of Elders. You see Roy Jones Jr. move from middleweight into light heavyweight. Elon Musk moved from Zip2 to PayPal to Tesla to SpaceX. Martha Stewart moved from lifestyle, to cooking, to furniture, to home appliances. Fred Dalton moved from professional actor to Senator. Sheryl

Sandberg moved from VP of Global Sales and Operations at Google, to COO at Facebook, and then to NY Times bestselling author. Schwarzenegger moved from bodybuilding, to acting, and then to being the Governor of California.

Now it's true that this type of high level achiever is the exception and not the norm. Most of the world's most productive people are so because of the fact that they have found and mastered one specific craft and never looked back. However, for some of them, it's not enough to master one thing. Some of them need to continue to challenge themselves to expand, grow, and learn. If this is you then it's valid to move on to the next challenge in order to keep yourself in a continual state of expansion. However, this is different than jumping from vocation to vocation without ever having achieved anything meaningful. Rather, this is the polar opposite where, upon total mastery of one craft, it is deemed that taking on another will continue to expand the consciousness of the individual. In this instance there is validity to continual transition upon mastery of the current trajectory.

Again, for the majority of the world's most productive people on the planet, most of their time and energy is dedicated towards mastering one craft and becoming the very best in the world at it. This should remain as your objective and only change after you have come into complete and total mastery of your current one. Even then, you should only shift directions if you really, really want to and you've really, really mastered the one thing. Otherwise, keep the course and continue to reap the amazing rewards of being the best in the world at what you do.

The point is that you will need to continue to challenge yourself to stay in a constant state of expansion. This means that the goal will never be to get it done or to be finished. Sure, there will be objectives and milestones along the way and you will wish to acknowledge the completion of these. However, your mission is to keep the creative energy going and a quintessential element of this is accepting that you will never be finished. There is no *done*. There is only your powerful creative flow and incessant drive to be the best possible version of yourself that you can be in this lifetime.

Remember when we used to judge people in the media who were still doing what they loved even when they were in their 60's, 70's, and 80's?

"He's too old to still be doing that, what a joke!" My buddy said that to me about Sylvester Stallone when he started making the new Rocky and Rambo series simultaneously while in his 60's. I had mixed emotions about it at the time. My first thought was, "He's right, that's ridiculous." Then my second thought was, "No wait, that's amazing, this guy never gives up, never quits, and will continue doing what he loves no matter who says what about it."

The point is that I was about to fall into the "age limiting beliefs trap" which is another belief in a long line of limiting beliefs that we all share about the world. They are subconscious, mass-mind beliefs, that we have about the nature of reality. They are beliefs about what we should and should not do with our lives. They are beliefs about what we can and cannot do with our lives. They are beliefs about what we are and are not capable of doing. The most important thing about them is to realize that you have them. They are within your subconscious mind and they will attempt to validate any external idea that you cannot or should not achieve your dreams or goals.

What I did was to recognize that when I was judging Sylvester for doing what he loves to do, I was actually self-validating my own limiting beliefs about my own inability to do what I love to do. Another way of saying this is that, if I am judging someone else for doing what they love to do, I will probably not allow myself to do what I love to do either. If I judge someone for making a lot of money then I will probably not allow myself to make much money. And if I judge someone for being successful at what they do then I will probably not allow myself to ever achieve much success in my own life.

Age is just a number that means you've had a certain amount of life experience. It's no reason to quit thinking about the pursuit of your creative passion. If anything, the older you are, the more creativity you have to share with the world. When you believe that you are done because you've reached a certain age then, not only do you rob your Soul of its desire to continue to create, but you also rob the world of your wisdom and knowledge.

To be sure though, this line of thinking is not even an option for you. The world's most productive people simply do not think this way. Age never enters into the equation and, if anything, they will be doing what they love to do on the way to the cemetery. You may have to wait to lower them into the ground while they take a conference call.

Get the point?

You're never, ever done. You don't get it done and you will never be finished. This is because you've just shifted into a new gear which is a continual state of creativity, growth, and expansion.

Congratulations, you made it. Welcome to the ride; there are no stops.

Lesson 11: Integration

1. Good lord, do I even need to say this one? No, you will never retire, so get it out of your head right now. That is for the average person to work towards, the slow death. Your job is to continue to fire on all pistons and hit the turbo charger. There is no end in sight for you, and thank god.

2. You will continue to research, daydream, brainstorm, and be creative. Your goal is to continue to allow yourself to tap into the nonlinear domain of thought and bring your ideas into the world. Your goal is to continue to improve the quality of life on the planet.

3. If you are one of those very rare individuals who achieve complete and total mastery of your one craft, then it's okay to start something new. The desire to challenge yourself and expand your consciousness is valid. So start something new and continue to challenge yourself to be the best possible version of you that you can be.

CHRIS works with entrepreneurs, business owners, CEO's, actors, athletes, and artists all across the world every day via video & phone or in person in a one on one or team setting. He is happy to help with your extraordinary journey to reach the absolute highest level of human performance that you are capable of. If you need:

- Help expanding your thinking in order to see the larger picture and 10x your business growth

- Help prioritizing your goals so that you take only action-steps that create real, tangible results

- Help in becoming a magnetic, mindful leader who people admire, respect, and are naturally drawn to

- Help ending self sabotage cycles so that you can reach a level of success that you know in your heart you are capable of

- Help becoming aware of how you come across to others so that you can gain the respect and trust of your team and associates

- Help creating a peaceful atmosphere around you that naturally yields an accelerated level of productivity

- Help achieving the state of mind that is shared by all of the most productive people on the planet and leads to uncommon success

Then you should contact
Chris @ info@christopherpinckley.com
In the end, it's all a State of Mind.

Popular books by Chris:

Reality Creation 101
Alive Awake Aware
State of Mind 2.0
The Mud Removal Program.

www.ingramcontent.com/pod-product-compliance
Lightning Source LLC
Chambersburg PA
CBHW070236190526
45169CB00001B/202